# Contents

**Introduction: About this guide**   **3**

**The legislative framework**   **5**

Equality Act 2010   6
    Services, public functions and associations   6
    Employment   7
    Education   8
    Public sector Equality Duty   9
Building regulations   11
British Standard BS 8300   13
Access statements, access audits and access strategies   14

**Design guidance**   **17**

External environment   18

1 Car parking   18
2 Setting-down points   24
3 Pedestrian routes   25
4 Shared spaces   33
5 Street furniture   37
6 External ramps   39
7 External steps   43
8 Handrails   46

Internal environment   48

9 Entrances   48
10 Doors – external and internal   53
11 Doors – access control systems   59
12 Doors – opening and closing systems   60
13 Entrance foyers   67
14 Reception desks and service counters   70
15 Seating   73
16 Horizontal circulation   76
17 Surfaces   80
18 Internal ramps, steps, stairs and handrails   83

**Contents**

19 Passenger lifts                                    85
20 Platform lifts                                     89
21 Sanitary facilities                                94
22 Wayfinding, information and signs                  108
23 Communication systems and acoustics               114
24 Switches and controls                              119
25 Lighting                                           121

Building management                                   123

26 Building management checklist                      124
27 Means of escape                                    129

**Appendices**                                        **133**

Organisations                                         133
Publications                                          135
Index                                                 138

# Introduction: About this guide

Inclusive design is a fast-moving field and this, the third edition of *Designing for Accessibility*, brings together evolving legislation, updated guidance and current good practice in the design of public buildings and outdoor spaces. Its purpose is to promote good practice in the design and management of the built environment and to set out relevant information in a user-friendly format.

This 2012 edition of *Designing for Accessibility* has been extensively updated and extended in the context of the Equality Act 2010 and current fire safety legislation. It includes comprehensive detailed design guidance which is based primarily on the 2009 edition of BS 8300 *Design of buildings and their approaches to meet the needs of disabled people – Code of practice* as well as the current Building Regulations applicable to the four UK countries and from accumulated experience of good design practice. This edition includes completely new sections covering the design of shared spaces, Changing Places toilets, accessible baby changing facilities and light reflectance values.

The guidance in *Designing for Accessibility* will assist providers of services, employers and education providers to fulfil their duties under the Equality Act 2010. It will also assist all those responsible for the commissioning, design and development of the built environment as well as those who use and manage it. This may include architects, designers, facilities managers, developers, planning and building control officers, service providers and consumers.

*Designing for Accessibility* closely refers to a range of design standards, codes of practice and specifications, but should not be viewed as a substitute for these documents. Architects and designers should refer directly to all relevant documents in addition to using *Designing for Accessibility* when designing and specifying components of buildings, equipment and particular services.

There will be further changes in legislation and all those involved in the commissioning, design and management of buildings and the provision of services will need to keep themselves informed.

While *Designing for Accessibility* has no legal status, an architect's or designer's duty of care to a client will be demonstrated by following good practice guidance contained in it.

**Note:** In all figures, measurements are in mm, unless otherwise stated.

# The legislative framework

- Equality Act 2010

- Building Regulations

- British Standard BS 8300

- Access statements, access audits
  and access strategies

# Equality Act 2010

In England, Scotland and Wales, the Equality Act 2010 (the Act) replaced pre-existing anti-discrimination legislation with a single Act. The Act unified legislation which previously covered different aspects of discrimination separately. Previous legislation including the Disability Discrimination Acts 1995 and 2005 are now repealed. (In Northern Ireland, the Disability Discrimination Act 1995 and other single-issue equality legislation still applies.)

The Act protects the rights of individuals and enhances equality of opportunity for all. The aim of the Act is to promote a fair and equal society and to protect individuals from unfair discrimination and treatment in all aspects of everyday life. It also sets a new standard for public service providers who are expected to embed equality issues into all aspects of public service delivery and to treat everyone with dignity and respect.

The Act protects individuals from discrimination on a range of grounds which it refers to as 'protected characteristics'. These are:

- Age
- Disability
- Gender reassignment
- Marriage and civil partnership
- Pregnancy and maternity
- Race
- Religion or belief
- Sex and sexual orientation

The Act simplified and strengthened the law and introduced new measures to protect people from dual discrimination, direct discrimination, indirect discrimination, discrimination arising from a disability, harassment and victimisation. People who experience direct discrimination or harassment because they are associated with a person who has a protected characteristic are also now protected under the Act, as are people who are mistakenly believed to have a protected characteristic.

Most of the Act, including measures to protect against direct and indirect discrimination, victimisation and harassment when accessing services, facilities (buildings) and public functions, employment, education, membership of associations and transport, came into force on 1 October 2010. Other aspects of the Act including the public sector Equality Duty came into effect in April 2011.

## Services, public functions and associations

Part 3 of the Act sets out provisions to protect people from discrimination when accessing services and public functions, whether provided in the public or private sector and whether they are paid for or not. Part 7 of the Act sets out provisions relating to membership associations. Where the term 'service provider' is used in the paragraphs below it refers all providers of services, whether this be to the general public, members, associates or guests, across both parts of the Act.

Under the Act, service providers have a duty to make reasonable adjustments to ensure that disabled people (including actual and potential service users or members of associations or guests) are not substantially disadvantaged when compared with non-disabled people. The measure of what is 'reasonable' under the Act is now more onerous and it is likely that service providers will have to make more adjustments than under previous legislation. The duty requires service providers to take positive steps that will ensure disabled people are able to enjoy a comparable degree of access to a service as that enjoyed by the public generally.

The duty to make reasonable adjustments applies to policies and procedures, physical features and the provision of auxiliary aids and services. Determination of what is a reasonable adjustment will vary depending on individual circumstances, but will include a consideration of the cost, practicality, extent of disruption while making the adjustment, the potential benefit to other service users and the resources available to the particular organisation.

The Act requires service providers to be proactive in identifying potential barriers to disabled people and to have a plan of action to reduce or eliminate these. The duty to make reasonable adjustments is a continuing duty and service providers are expected to continually review their response in the light of experience and feedback from service users.

Under the Act, service providers are permitted to use positive action when meeting the particular needs of people who access their goods, facilities or services. Positive action is when a service provider actively targets a group of people that has particular needs, is under-represented in terms of current service users, or is disadvantaged. This is a voluntary option – there is no duty for service providers to take positive action.

The positive action provisions under the Act apply to all the protected characteristics, but differ slightly in the way they are applied to disabled people. Disabled people can lawfully be treated more favourably than non-disabled people under the Act, but it is also lawful for people with a particular disability to be treated more favourably than people with a different disability.

## Employment

Part 5 of the Act sets out provisions to protect people against discrimination in the workplace, when they are seeking work and during dismissal.

A cornerstone of the Act is the duty for employers to make reasonable adjustments to ensure that disabled people can access and progress in employment. This is much more than a duty simply to avoid treating disabled people unfavourably – it requires positive additional steps to ensure disabled people are able to pursue employment opportunities and relates to measures to which non-disabled employees (and prospective employees) are not entitled.

Reasonable adjustments may include arrangements to enable a disabled person to attend an interview or to undertake aspects of their job. It may relate to adjustments in working arrangements, policies and procedures or to the provision of auxiliary aids. It also relates to physical alterations to features in buildings to enable access to the working environment and the use of any facilities provided for employees.

The duty to make reasonable adjustments applies to all employers, no matter how large or small the organisation. It is likely that what is considered reasonable for a small organisation to do will differ from what is expected of a large organisation as the individual circumstances of employers vary widely.

Employers are able (but not required) to take 'positive action' under the Act in relation to all aspects of employment such as recruitment, promotion, transfer, training and development, in order to encourage greater take-up amongst under-represented or disadvantaged groups. The Act also makes it lawful for employers to treat a disabled person more favourably than a non-disabled person.

Although not required by law, it is good practice for employers to have an Equality Policy which sets out the organisation's commitment to equality and includes a plan of action, the names of staff with specific responsibility for equality issues and any practical measures such as the delivery of equality training.

## Education

Part 6 of the Act sets out provisions to protect people against discrimination in all aspects of education. The duties for education providers relate to existing as well as prospective pupils and students and to former students (in limited circumstances). The duties support the agenda of improving education and attainment as a precursor to better opportunities and greater independence in adult life.

The provisions under the Act differ for schools and for providers of further and higher education.

In schools, the Act introduces a duty to provide auxiliary aids and services where a disabled pupil would otherwise be at a substantial disadvantage. This duty sits alongside existing duties under Part 4 of the Education Act 1996 through which pupils may already receive support under the special educational needs (SEN) framework. The new duties cover situations such as when a disabled pupil does not have a special educational needs statement but does require reasonable adjustments (or when the statement doesn't provide for auxiliary aids) in order to fully participate in learning and wider educational activities. The duty to make reasonable adjustments does not relate to physical features as this is covered by the accessibility planning duties. The reasonable adjustment duty will come into force at a later date following a period of consultation on implementation and approach.

Further and higher education providers have a duty to make reasonable adjustments to ensure that disabled students are able to access and participate in all aspects of learning and are not placed at a substantial disadvantage because of an arrangement, criterion or practice, physical barrier or absence of an auxiliary aid or services. The duty requires education providers to take positive steps to ensure that disabled students are able to fully participate and enjoy the other benefits, facilities and services associated with their education.

Schools and providers of further and higher education are also able to take voluntary positive action under the Act to address inequality, disadvantage and under-representation.

The duty to make reasonable adjustments (for schools and further and higher education providers) is a continuing and anticipatory duty.

## Public sector Equality Duty

The public sector Equality Duty, as set out in section 149 of the Act, came into force on 5 April 2011 and replaced the previous gender, disability and race equality duties. It applies to all public bodies listed in Schedule 19 of the Act and to any other organisation when it is carrying out a public function. The list of public bodies includes central government departments, local authorities, district and parish councils, court and criminal justice services, health, education and transport bodies, and emergency services as well as many others. The Equality Duty applies across England, Scotland and Wales.

Implementation of the Equality Duty will ensure public bodies are playing their part in making society fairer. The aims of the Equality Duty are threefold:

- to eliminate unlawful discrimination, victimisation and harassment
- to promote equality of opportunity for all
- to foster good relations, promote understanding and challenge prejudice.

The aims of the Equality Duty should be uppermost in the decision making process for all public bodies. The Equality Duty is a continuing duty, which means that its aims should be considered when policies or services are in development, during any decision making stages, when policies are implemented or services brought into action and during follow-up review. Where third parties are involved in delivering services on behalf of a public body, the public body is responsible for ensuring the third party is able to comply with the Equality Duty.

In undertaking the Equality Duty, public bodies may use the positive action provisions to treat some people more favourably than others, where this is permitted under the Act.

The Equality Duty is underpinned by Specific Duties which came into force in September 2011 under the Equality Act 2010 (Specific Duties) Regulations 2011. The Specific Duties require organisations to publish information about how they are meeting the Equality Duty, with the aim of improving performance and accountability. They require organisations to publish:

- equality objectives, at intervals of no more than every four years
- information demonstrating their compliance with the Equality Duty, at least every year.

# Building regulations

## England and Wales

In England and Wales, building design and construction are governed by the Building Regulations (see page 12 for Scotland and Northern Ireland). These regulations comprise a series of requirements for specific purposes: health and safety, energy conservation, prevention of contamination of water and the welfare and convenience of persons in or about buildings.

Building Regulations are supported by 'Approved Documents' which give practical guidance with respect to meeting the regulations. While their use is not mandatory – and the requirements of regulations can be met in other ways – Approved Documents are a valuable benchmarking tool.

Following the transfer of power for making building regulations to the Welsh Ministers on 31 December 2011, changes to building regulations and associated guidance in either England or Wales will relate only to the country in which the changes are made. The existing building regulations and approved documents will apply in both countries until changes are made and new guidance issued.

The principal parts of the Buildings Regulations that affect the accessibility of buildings, and their supporting Approved Documents, are as follows:

### Part M: Access to and use of buildings

Part M of the Building Regulations sets minimum legal standards for access and use of buildings by everyone, including disabled people. Since a requirement for access was first introduced in 1985, there have been a number of changes to and extensions in the scope of access regulations. In 2004, Part M was revised to foster a more inclusive approach and titled 'Access to and use of buildings'. The wording of the regulation avoids specific reference to, and a definition of, disabled people. This inclusive approach means that buildings and their facilities should be accessible and usable by everyone, including parents with children, older people and disabled people.

Part M applies to non-domestic buildings and dwellings, although separate requirements apply to each. For non-domestic buildings, the requirements apply to new buildings, alterations to existing buildings and certain changes of use.

### Approved Document M

Approved Document M (AD M) 2004 includes technical guidance on providing access to and within buildings. It was informed by the British Standard applicable at the time of issue, which was BS 8300:2001 *Design of buildings and their approaches to meet the needs of disabled people – Code of practice* (see page 13). Dimensional criteria in AD M are largely, but not entirely, in accordance with BS 8300.

### Part K Protection from falling, collision and impact

Part K of the building regulations sets minimum legal standards for stairs, ladders, ramps and guarding in domestic and non-domestic buildings.

### Approved Document K

In April 2013, guidance covering internal stairs and ramps which form part of a building as well as guidance covering door vision panels and manifestation markings transfers from AD M into a new edition of Approved Document K (AD K). AD K also incorporates all existing guidance previously covered by AD N Glazing. The 2013 Edition of AD K applies in England only.

### Part B: Fire safety

Part B of the Building Regulations sets minimum legal standards for means of warning and escape from a fire. Part B applies to non-domestic buildings and dwellings.

### Approved Document B

Approved Document B (AD B) includes technical guidance on ensuring early warning systems and the design of means of escape are inclusive and meet the needs of everyone who is likely to use buildings, including disabled people. Volume 1 of AD B covers dwelling houses. Volume 2 (covering buildings other than dwelling houses) provides guidance on evacuation lifts, accessible final exits, limitations on travel distances, phased evacuation, the provision of refuges, the use of vision panels in doors on escape routes and the provision of suitable warning devices for hearing impaired people.

## Scotland

In Scotland, access requirements are integrated across the Building Regulations. Practical guidance on meeting the provisions of the Building Regulations is available in the 2011 Technical Handbooks; there are two volumes, *Domestic buildings and Non-domestic buildings*, each of which has seven sections covering structure, fire, environment, safety, noise, energy and sustainability.

## Northern Ireland

In Northern Ireland, Part R of the Building Regulations (NI) covers access to and use of buildings, and is supported by Technical Booklet R: 2006. Fire safety is covered in Part E and supported by Technical Booklet E: 2005.

# British Standard BS 8300

BS 8300:2009 *Design of buildings and their approaches to meet the needs of disabled people – Code of practice* provides comprehensive detailed guidance on how buildings and their surroundings can be designed to facilitate convenient access and use by disabled people. The guidance reflects the fact that disabled people may be visitors or customers, service users, staff or volunteers, residents, spectators or members of an audience, participants or holders of public office and that accessibility is relevant to all building types.

Many of the design recommendations in BS 8300, which was first published in 2001, were based for the first time on ergonomic research. Amendments to the standard, principally covering door closing forces and visual contrast, were issued in 2005. Further developments covered by the second edition (2009) include additional detailed guidance on using light reflectance values to assess visual contrast, information on the slip potential characteristics of floor finishes and amendments to space allowances data. Also included for the first time are recommendations and detailed guidance on the provision of Changing Places sanitary accommodation in larger buildings used by the general public (see page 94).

BS 8300 includes commentary which provides a context and rationale for the design guidance. Management and maintenance issues are incorporated in recognition that these play an essential part in ensuring the accessibility of services and facilities to disabled people.

The recommendations in the standard apply to car parking provision, setting-down points and garaging, access routes to and around all buildings, lifts and platform lifts, and entrances to and interiors of new buildings. Where relevant, the guidance in BS 8300 has informed the design guidance in the Approved Document M (AD M) of the Building Regulations, although there are some differences between the two documents. The scope of BS 8300 is far broader than that of AD M and it usefully provides guidance on many features of buildings that fall outside the remit of building control.

The guidance in BS 8300 forms a suitable basis for assessing the accessibility and usability of existing buildings and, where practicable, as a basis for their improvement.

# Access statements, access audits and access strategies

Planning for accessibility requires a methodical approach and is pertinent to all stages in the life-cycle of a building. When a new development is being planned, provision for access should be considered from the outset and recorded in project briefing material, feasibility proposals and in any access statements required to accompany formal submissions such as planning and Building Regulations applications. Access audits are most relevant to existing buildings as a means of identifying potential barriers to access, while access strategies set out a plan of action for future changes, whether they are in the short or longer term. Each is described in more detail below.

## Access statements

An access statement is a description of how inclusive design principles and practice are incorporated into a particular project or development, and subsequently maintained and managed. An access statement is not a static document but a living process which evolves with the scheme, from initially being fairly generic to gradually becoming more specific and detailed. Access statements are of benefit and relevance to designers, contractors, planning, building control and access officers, building owners and managers and local access groups.

Design and access statements, describing how a design has evolved and how it incorporates provisions for access, are required to accompany many applications for outline and full planning consent. *Design and access statements: How to write, read and use them* published by CABE in 2006 provides comprehensive detailed guidance with the aim of creating high-quality places that are accessible to all.

A key process in the development of a design and access statement is involvement and consultation. Designers and developers are encouraged to undertake professional consultations and involve the local community at an early stage, and should set out in their design and access statement who they have consulted (or propose to consult) and the outcomes. Involvement and consultation with access groups and the local community is encouraged and expected for major developments and significant projects to which the general public will be admitted.

Access statements are also applicable to the Building Regulations process and provide a means of highlighting (and justifying) situations in which design solutions vary from guidance contained in AD M. In the case of existing buildings, particularly historic buildings, an access statement enables the designer or developer to identify the constraints posed by the existing structure and its immediate environment and to propose compensatory measures where full access proves to be impracticable or only achievable at disproportionate cost.

Access statements that accompany Building Regulations applications should be seen as complementary to, and as a development of, that which is provided for planning purposes, rather than as a separate document.

Access statements also provide an audit trail to demonstrate whether particular matters have been considered adequately and with the benefit of current and authoritative guidance. Their use can help guard against the danger of routine maintenance or minor alterations compromising access provisions that have been specifically designed in.

It is beneficial to maintain and update access statements as building projects progress in order to provide the end user of the building, who may have ongoing obligations under the Equality Act 2010, with a record of the evolution of design and any relevant management decisions.

## Access audits

Access audits provide a 'snapshot' of an existing building at a particular point in time. In broad terms, an access audit is an assessment of a particular building or environment in terms of accessibility. Access audits are a useful starting point when assessing a building's current state of accessibility and usability, particularly when improvements are planned. Recommendations arising from an access audit can be used as a basis for a programme of stand-alone access improvements or to highlight elements that should be incorporated into a larger building improvement project.

The scope of access audits may vary depending on the client's particular requirements and nature of the building or organisation being assessed. However, as a general principle, access audits should cover not only how people approach, access and use buildings and the facilities within them, but also how people leave buildings, particularly in the event of a fire.

The CAE / RIBA Publishing *Access Audit Handbook* 2nd edition will be published early in 2013 and will provide detailed guidance on undertaking access audits and report writing.

## Access strategies

Access strategies (also termed access plans) are the best way of ensuring that information gathered and recommendations arising from access audits are effectively used. Access strategies should include a plan of action for implementing changes and may record information such as timescales, approvals, funding and lines of responsibility, particularly where physical changes are required. Access strategies should be regularly reviewed and updated if necessary, since even without major structural adaptations, buildings and the way they are used change over time. Access strategies should take a long-term view of improving access and identify opportunities for change (for example at routine maintenance or when a major refit is planned), demonstrating a serious commitment to making buildings more accessible to everyone. They should cover policies, procedures, practices and management; provision of equipment and auxiliary aids and services; and the physical environment.

# Design guidance

- External environment

- Internal environment

# External environment

## 1 Car parking

Cars are an essential means of transport for many disabled people, both as drivers and as passengers. So too are taxis, door-to-door accessible transport vehicles, adapted commercial vehicles and minibuses. The provision of suitable car parking facilities for vehicles as well as space for motorists to drop off and collect passengers are essential to provide easy access to public buildings and workplaces.

The level of parking provision will depend on many factors including location, function and size of the building and site. New car parks should be designed to accommodate future changes to the number and type of bays in response to the likely changing needs of the workforce and local population.

Where on-site parking is not available, it is good practice to maintain a record of nearby designated parking bays such as on-street bays and in off-street car parks. In addition, and if space is available, an approach could be made to the local authority for the provision of on-street parking as near as possible to the building or site.

- *Table 1.1* sets out the recommended minimum number of designated parking bays for disabled staff and visitors as well as additional recommended provision such as enlarged standard and designated bays.

- Where parking is provided, at least one bay designated for disabled people should be provided as close as possible to the principal entrance of the building.

- There are circumstances where, even when there is no standard parking provision, designated accessible parking may be needed.

- The location of designated parking bays should be clearly signposted from the car park entrance and at each change in direction (or change in level) within the car park.

- Allow for future expansion in the number of designated parking bays by providing a number of larger standard bays, 3.6m wide × 6m long (see *Table 1.1*). In the interim, these bays will benefit people who need additional space getting into and out of vehicles.

- Where space is available, provide a large designated parking space for use by commercial vehicles such as minibuses with integral side and rear hoist access, 4.8m wide × 8m long.

**Table 1.1**
**Minimum recommended number of bays in off street car parks**

|  | **Staff** | **Visitors** | **Enlarged standard spaces** |
|---|---|---|---|
| Workplaces | One space for each employee who is a disabled motorist | 5 per cent of total car park capacity | 5 per cent of total capacity |
| Shopping, leisure and recreation | One space for each employee who is a disabled motorist | 6 per cent of total car park capacity | 4 per cent of total capacity |
| Railway stations | One space for each employee who is a disabled motorist | 5 per cent of total car park capacity | 5 per cent of total capacity |
| Religious buildings and crematoria | – | Minimum 2 spaces or 6 per cent of total car park capacity (whichever is greater) | 4 per cent of total capacity |
| Sports facilities | Sport England recommends a minimum of 8 spaces, or 8 per cent (whichever is greater) for some sports facilities and for 50 metre pools Refer to *Accessible Sports Facilities* published by Sport England for detailed guidance relating to different types of sports facilities | | |
| All facilities | Where space permits, provide an additional large designated bay (4.8m wide x 8m long) for commercial vehicles with side and rear hoists | | |
| Where the function of the building means that a larger number of disabled people are expected, the numbers should be increased in order to meet anticipated need. | | | |

## Location and arrangement

• Off-street designated parking bays should be as close as possible to the principal entrance of the building or attraction it serves.

• If designated parking cannot be provided close to the entrance, the route between the parking bays and entrance should ideally be covered and have seating at intervals along the route.

• In multi-storey car parks, designated parking bays should ideally be at the same level as the principal (or alternative accessible) entrance or the main access route to and from the car park. Alternatively, a suitable passenger lift or ramp should be provided. Designated bays are best grouped together so they are easier to find and to manage.

• Dimensions for designated parking bays and access zones are illustrated in *Figure 1.1*.

• Designated parking bays should be level (subject to a gradient and cross-fall no greater than 1:50).

Figure 1.1
**Designated off-street parking bays**

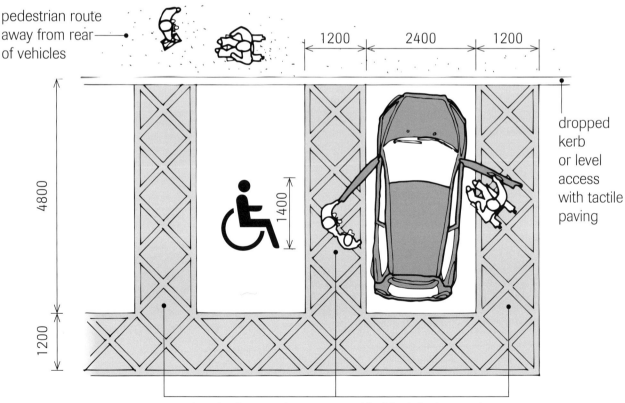

pedestrian route away from rear of vehicles

1200    2400    1200

4800

1200

1400

dropped kerb or level access with tactile paving

hatched zones between and behind designated bays for side and rear access

- The route between designated parking spaces, ticket machines, car park or storey exits (such as in multi-storey car parks) and the building entrance should be accessible and clearly identified.

- All pedestrian routes within the car park should be level or with shallow gradients (see also *Pedestrian routes,* page 25). Kerbs between the parking area and routes to buildings should be dropped to provide easy access for wheelchair users, with tactile warnings where appropriate (see the Department for Transport's Guidance on the use of Tactile Paving Surfaces).

- Surface materials for designated bays and access routes should be firm, smooth and even and free from loose stones. (See also *Pedestrian routes,* page 25.)

- Designated bays should be clearly identified with a ground-painted symbol (1400mm high) as well as a wall- or post-mounted sign positioned 1000mm above ground level.

- Artificial lighting should be provided to designated parking areas and along access routes to buildings, giving an even level of illumination of 20 lux. (Steps and ramps should be 100 lux.)

## Barriers, control systems and ticket machines

- Height barriers to car parks should provide a vertical clearance of 2.6m. This clearance should be maintained along all routes between the car park entrance, designated parking bays and exits.

- Advance warning of height restrictions should be clearly visible. Where the vertical clearance is less than 2.6m in existing car parks, signage to nearby alternative designated parking should be displayed.

- In private car parks, where an access-control system is required, the system should be easily accessible to all potential users. Remote-control systems are recommended or proximity / swipe card systems with dual-height readers.

- Information indicating whether or not free parking is available to disabled motorists should be provided at the car park entrance.

- Ticket-dispensing machines such as are commonly found at car park entrances should be usable by all motorists without having to leave their vehicle.

- Ticket-dispensing and payment machines such as in pay-and-display car parks should be accessible to all motorists. If only one machine is provided, the controls should be between 750mm and 1200mm above ground level (see *Figure 1.2*). Where more than one machine is provided, the others may have controls at a higher level (between 1000mm and 1400mm).

- Clear unobstructed access should be maintained in front of ticket machines and they should be located on level ground. Any plinth or kerb should not project in front of the machine as this may impede access.

Figure 1.2
**Accessible ticket-dispensing machine**

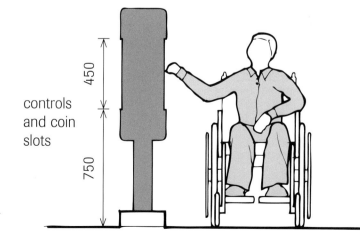
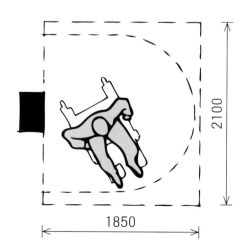

controls and coin slots

450

750

2100

1850

## On-street parking

• On-street designated parking bays should be arranged to enable safe access via both sides and the rear of a vehicle. See *Figure 1.3* for dimensions.

• A dropped kerb or level surface with blister tactile paving should be provided to one end of the bay to enable access to a vehicle using a ramp or tail lift. The kerb edging to the side of the bay enables transfer via side-entry vehicles.

• Setting-down points should be located on level ground (subject to a gradient and cross-fall no greater than 1:50).

Figure 1.3
**Designated on-street parking bay**

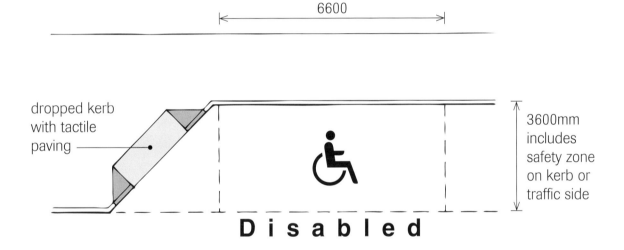

# 2 Setting-down points

The provision of a suitable setting-down point enables passengers to be dropped off and picked up close to the entrance to a building. This is particularly important where there is no on-site car park or if the car park is located some distance from the building entrance.

Setting-down points enable a driver to park temporarily, assist a disabled companion to alight from a vehicle and enter the building before returning to the vehicle. Similarly, they enable a driver to park temporarily whilst meeting a disabled person from the building and accompanying them back to the vehicle.

• Setting-down points should be clearly signposted and located on level ground as near to the main entrance (or alternative accessible entrance) as possible.

• A separate setting-down / waiting area for taxis and dial-a-ride vehicles is recommended, as is a short-term waiting area for drivers waiting to collect disabled passengers (or a disabled driver waiting to collect passengers), where space permits.

• The surface of the footway should be level with the carriageway at the setting-down point, to allow convenient transfer to and from a wheelchair.

• A section of the footpath with a kerb should be usable as a setting-down point for people transferring into and out of taxis and other vehicles using integral fold-out ramps.

• Wherever possible, setting-down points should be protected from the weather.

# 3 Pedestrian routes

Pedestrian routes within a site provide essential access to and around buildings, car parks and other external facilities. Routes may also be an amenity themselves such as paths across a park or campus. Many pedestrian routes leading to principal and alternative building entrances are also designated emergency egress routes. All such routes should be accessible and safe for everyone to use.

Changes in level are difficult for many people to negotiate. As far as is practical, access should be level or near level from the edge of the site or from designated accessible car parking spaces to the main entrance and / or other entrances and other principal routes around and between buildings.

## Layout and gradients

• Route widths should be sufficient for people, including wheelchair users, to pass others travelling in the opposite direction. A width of 1800mm can accommodate any amount of non-vehicular traffic without the need for passing places; 1500mm in addition to passing places is acceptable on less busy routes; a width of 1200mm may be acceptable in exceptional circumstances on restricted sites and for a distance of no more than 2m (see *Figure 3.1*, page 26 for path dimensions and *Figure 3.2*, page 27 for passing places).

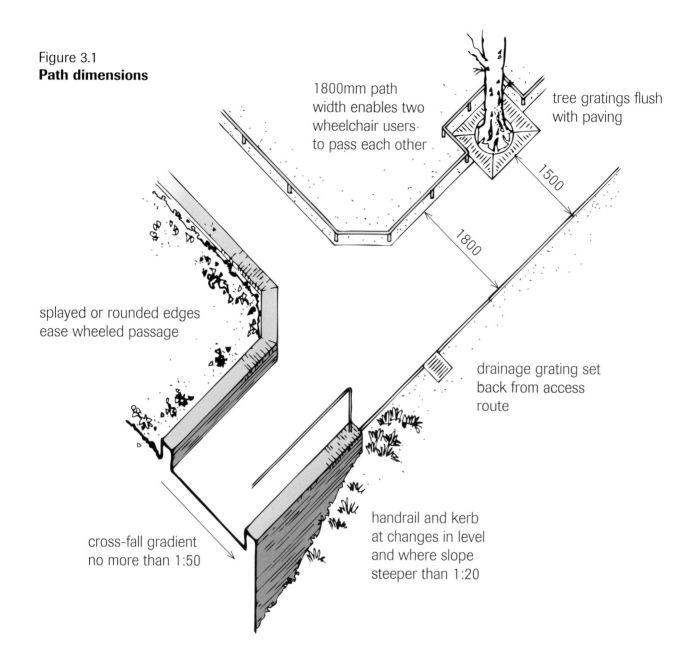

Figure 3.1
**Path dimensions**

1800mm path width enables two wheelchair users to pass each other

tree gratings flush with paving

1500

1800

splayed or rounded edges ease wheeled passage

drainage grating set back from access route

cross-fall gradient no more than 1:50

handrail and kerb at changes in level and where slope steeper than 1:20

- Passing places, where required, should be provided at all junctions and corners of an access route and at intervals of no more than 25m (or closer in order for one passing place to be within sight of another).

- Passing places should be at least 1.8m wide and 2m long (or 2.5m long in some sports facilities).

- Resting places with seating should be provided not more than 50m apart. Seats should be set back from the access route and have a clear space to both sides, preferably 1.5m × 1.5m, as in *Figure 3.2* (see also *Seating*, page 73).

- A clear height of 2.1m should be maintained to the full width of all access routes.

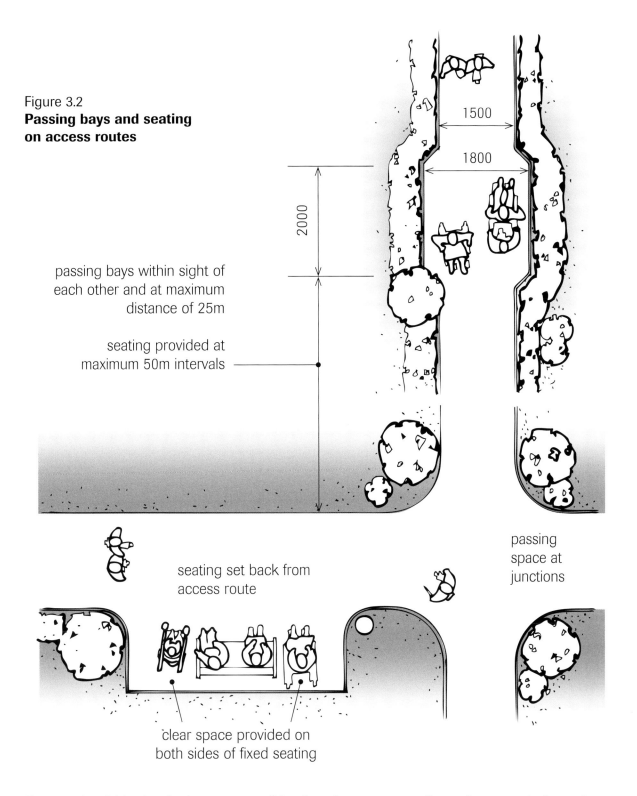

Figure 3.2
**Passing bays and seating
on access routes**

1500

1800

2000

passing bays within sight of
each other and at maximum
distance of 25m

seating provided at
maximum 50m intervals

seating set back from
access route

passing
space at
junctions

clear space provided on
both sides of fixed seating

- Routes should be level wherever possible. (Level means a gradient of 1:60 or shallower.) Where this is not possible, routes should be gently sloping. (Gently sloping means a gradient steeper than 1:60 but less than 1:20.)

- Gently sloping routes should incorporate a level landing after each 500mm rise and at each change in direction or junction.

- Where sections of the route require a gradient of 1:20 or steeper, the design guidance on external ramps applies (see page 39).

• Routes should have a cross-fall gradient no greater than 1:50 (except at dropped kerbs) to ensure rainwater is adequately drained.

• Routes should be clearly signed, and may include landmarks and features to aid orientation. These could include visual, audible and olfactory clues such as fountains and fragrant planting. Avoid clutter and consider the navigable building line used by guide dog users.

## Surfaces and drainage

• Surface materials should be firm, durable, reasonably smooth and slip-resistant in all weather (such as tarmac or York paving). Undulations in the surface should not exceed 3mm under a 1m straight edge for formless materials (such as tarmac, concrete and bonded gravel). All surface materials should be well laid and maintained.

• Surfaces such as sand, loose gravel, topsoil, cobbles and terrazzo should be avoided.

• Different surface materials offer different sound qualities, textures, colours and light reflectance. These can be used creatively to define sections of the route and to highlight particular features.

• Where a variety of surface materials are used along access routes, materials should have similar frictional characteristics so as not to present a tripping hazard.

• Drainage channels should be positioned outside of the access route if possible. If set within the access route, they should be flush with the surface and designed to avoid trapping walking aids and wheels. Ensure regular maintenance to avoid blockages and subsequent water pooling (see *Figure 3.3*).

• Joints between adjacent paving units and between paving units and utility covers should be detailed as follows:

  – for filled joints, a maximum 5mm level difference

  – for recessed joints, a maximum 2mm level difference, with joints no deeper than 5mm and no wider than 10mm

  – for unfilled joints, a maximum 2mm level difference, with joints no wider than 5mm.

Figure 3.3
**Flush drainage to paved surfaces**

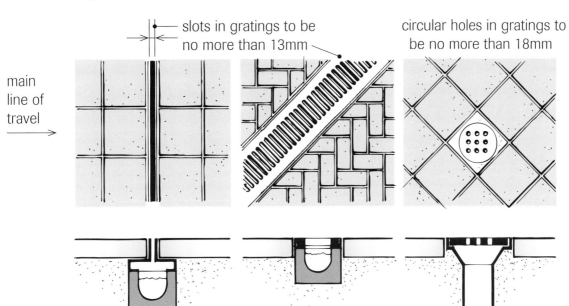

slots in gratings to be no more than 13mm

circular holes in gratings to be no more than 18mm

main line of travel →

## Signage and lighting

• Signs should be carefully located, clear, non-reflective and logical (see also *Wayfinding, information and signs*, page 108).

• Routes and potential hazards should be adequately lit. Artificial lighting should be designed to provide an even level of illumination. Low-level uplighters are not recommended because they may cause glare.

Figure 3.4
**Tactile paving surfaces**

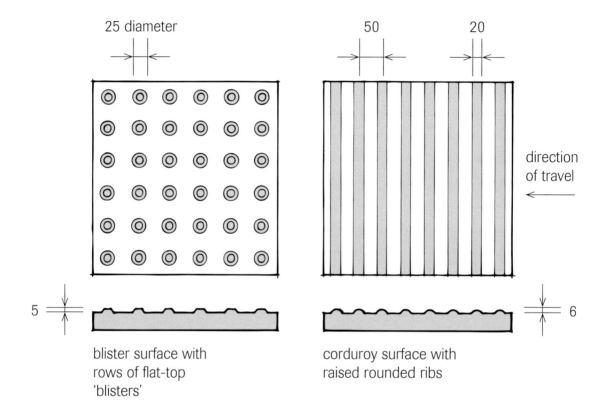

blister surface with
rows of flat-top
'blisters'

corduroy surface with
raised rounded ribs

## Hazard warning and protection

• Pedestrian and vehicular routes should be separated wherever possible and clearly differentiated.

• Blister tactile paving should be used to identify uncontrolled pedestrian crossing points. *Figure 3.5* shows the arrangement of blister tactile paving at uncontrolled crossing points where the pedestrian route is perpendicular to the vehicular route.

• Corduroy tactile hazard warning paving should be reserved for the top and bottom of external steps (see page 43).

• Hazard protection should be provided to any objects (for example open windows, outward-opening doors, ticket machines or planting boxes) that project more than 100mm onto an access route between a height of 300mm and 2100mm above the ground.

Figure 3.5
**Tactile paving at uncontrolled crossing points**

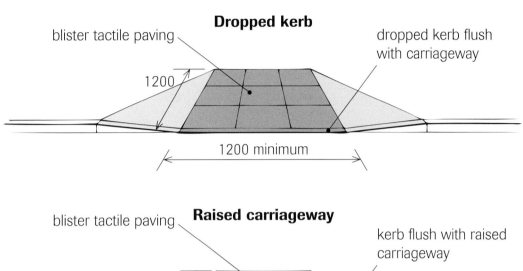

**Dropped kerb**

blister tactile paving

dropped kerb flush
with carriageway

1200

1200 minimum

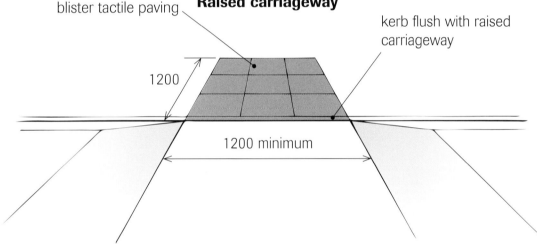

**Raised carriageway**

blister tactile paving

kerb flush with raised
carriageway

1200

1200 minimum

• Hazard protection should include guarding to each side of the object (900mm to 1100mm high) and a means of cane detection such as a kerb, solid barrier or tapping rail, as in *Figure 3.6.*

• Tapping rails should either be flush with the front face of the projecting object or set back no more than 100mm, and the underside of tapping rails should be no higher than 150mm above the ground.

• All potential obstructions and guarding should contrast visually with their surroundings.

Figure 3.6
**Hazard protection**

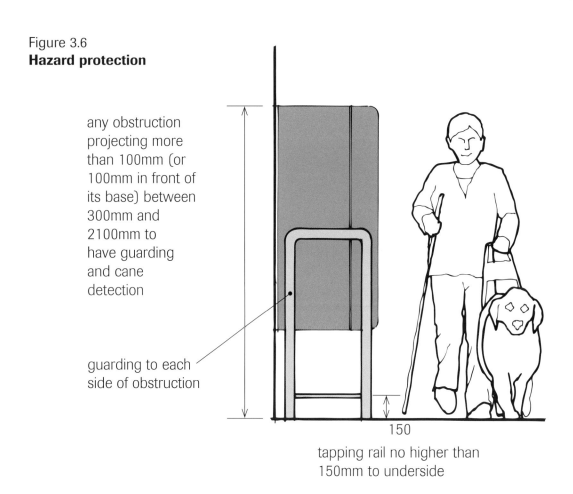

any obstruction projecting more than 100mm (or 100mm in front of its base) between 300mm and 2100mm to have guarding and cane detection

guarding to each side of obstruction

150

tapping rail no higher than 150mm to underside

# 4 Shared spaces

Shared spaces in the public realm include high street and other urban environments and residential areas such as Home Zones.* Shared spaces are designed to improve the quality of the environment by increasing the sense of place and encouraging social interaction while maintaining the capacity for vehicle and pedestrian movement along a route. Shared spaces reduce the dominance of vehicles and improve access, safety and amenity for pedestrians.

Shared spaces work best at low traffic volumes and speeds, and current research shows that vehicles are more likely to give way to pedestrians at speeds of 15mph or lower. At higher traffic volumes and speeds more defined measures need to be taken to ensure safety and convenience of pedestrians, especially when crossing the space.

The layout of shared spaces and the appropriate use of features such as landscaping, seating, artwork and cafés within the shared space (not just at the sides of streets) encourages the use of all areas by pedestrians as well as reducing traffic speed and modifying driver behaviour. In shared spaces, there is less formal differentiation between vehicular and pedestrian areas.

Some shared spaces have a shared surface (where there are no kerbs), but this is not an essential criterion. In shared spaces, the sides of streets often remain pedestrian-only areas (comfort space) while the central area is shared by pedestrians and vehicles.

The principles of inclusive design should be adopted for all shared space schemes and the needs of all pedestrians should be fully considered at each stage in the design process. There should be an emphasis on stakeholder engagement throughout the design and implementation process.

The guidance below highlights features of shared spaces that will improve accessibility for all users.

The chapters *Pedestrian routes* (see page 25), *Street furniture* (see page 37) and *Seating* (see page 73) are also relevant to the design of shared spaces.

---

* Home Zones are residential areas in which the layout and features of external spaces balance the needs of vehicular traffic with those of pedestrians, cyclists, residents and others users. See *Home Zones: A planning and design handbook.*

## Layout and features

• The layout of shared spaces should be logical and easy to interpret.

• The use of features such as sculpture, distinctive buildings, vistas and other features should be considered to help people orientate themselves and identify particular locations.

• Consider the need for a gateway feature to indicate the entrance to a shared space area, such as a change in surface material, a narrowing of road width or a raised carriageway area.

• Ensure courtesy crossing points are highlighted such as by using visual contrast, by changing the surface material, narrowing the vehicular approach area or locating the crossing on a raised table. Courtesy crossing points should be provided at regular intervals, appropriate to the location and distance covered by the shared space.

• The location of bus stops should be carefully considered to ensure they are easy to identify, are safe for waiting passengers and, where necessary, incorporate a raised kerb.

• Where kerbs delineate the edge of the comfort space, a locally raised kerb should be provided to facilitate level access onto and off buses. Where there is a level surface, a locally raised kerb should be provided, with gently sloping surfaces (no greater than 1:20) to street level.

Figure 4.1
**Features of shared spaces**

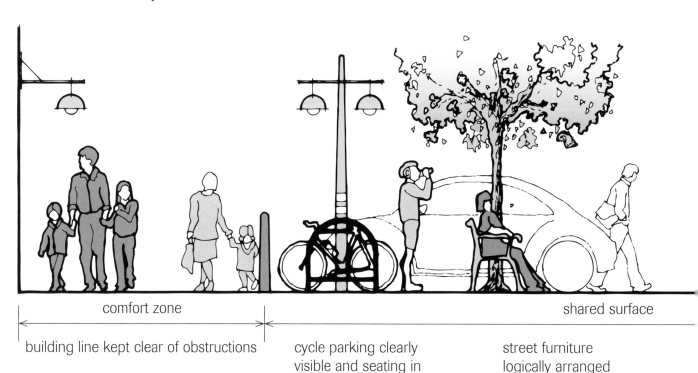

comfort zone                                                                                    shared surface

building line kept clear of obstructions          cycle parking clearly            street furniture
                                                  visible and seating in           logically arranged
                                                  safe locations

• The building line should be retained and kept free of obstructions, including temporary signs, café tables and chairs and shop sale items. All items of street furniture including planting, seats, cycle stands, parking meters, lighting, traffic and parking signs should be carefully positioned to minimise clutter and to ensure clear pedestrian zones are maintained.

• Where provided, comfort zones should be continuous between junctions and link with designated crossing points.

• Where level surfaces (kerb-free) are provided, the notional carriageway should be clearly differentiated from the comfort space using alternative means such as suitable placement of street furniture, bollards or a tactile delineator strip. A corduroy tactile strip is an acceptable delineator, which should change to blister paving at suggested crossing points.

• Research shows that 60mm is the lowest kerb that is detected by many visually impaired people.

• Surfaces should be free of clutter and provide ample space for general circulation as well as space that encourages social interaction, space for events such as markets or entertainment and for resting.

• Surfaces should be firm, relatively smooth and level. Cross-fall gradients in areas likely to be used as primary pedestrian routes should not exceed 1:50.

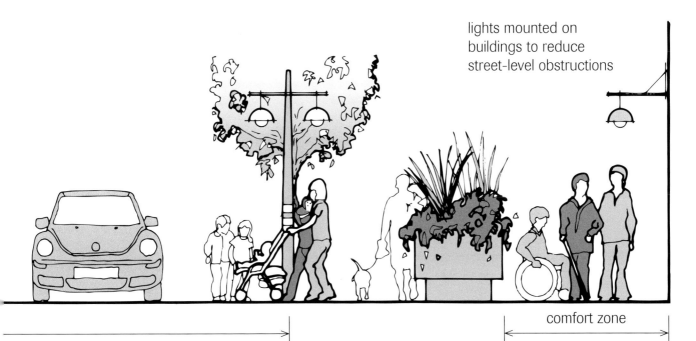

lights mounted on buildings to reduce street-level obstructions

comfort zone

surface materials used to differentiate between shared areas, parking bays and pedestrian-only areas

trees, lighting posts, planting tubs and bollards used to define edge of comfort zone

- Consider the use of surface materials that generate road noise when vehicles cross the surface where this may be beneficial as a means of alerting pedestrians.

- Use visual contrast to delineate between areas such as the comfort area and notional vehicle route, loading and parking bays, rest areas and seating, but avoid complex surface patterns which may cause visual confusion.

- Provide seating at regular intervals throughout the shared space, and positioned where people will feel safe and can enjoy the street environment.

- Consider the need for parking bays for Blue Badge holders within the shared space area. If provided, parking bays can be used to delineate comfort space and create road narrowing in order to encourage slower vehicle speeds.

- Artificial lighting should be provided throughout shared spaces to enhance safety for all road users, particularly pedestrians. An even level of illumination should be provided, with fittings selected and positioned to avoid glare and shadows.

- The positioning of lighting fittings should not cause clutter within the pedestrianised zone, but be integrated into the overall street design by being mounted on buildings and / or incorporated into other items of street furniture such as signs, shelters and bollards.

- Drainage design should be effective and ensure adequate run-off, particularly in level surface environments.

- For further guidance, see *Shared Space*.

# 5 Street furniture

Street furniture is an integral part of the pedestrian environment and contributes valuable directional guidance, resting places, litter collection, lighting and hazard warning. Ill-considered placement of street furniture causes obstructions, is potentially hazardous and looks unattractive. Good design and careful placement enhances the environment, improves safety and provides easier access for everyone.

- Street furniture should be positioned at or beyond the edge of pedestrian access routes so as not to cause an obstruction or hazard.

- If items of street furniture have to be located within access routes, they should be clearly identified, for example by contrasting visually with surrounding surfaces. Items such as bench seats which have open ends or sharp corners should be avoided.

- Consider the logical grouping of items such as seats and litter bins, signage and lighting and position all in convenient locations.

- Use visual contrast and / or changes in the texture of paving surfaces as well as effective lighting to define pedestrian routes.

- The provision of appropriate seating is important, especially on long or sloping routes and at junctions in routes (see also *Seating*, page 73).

- Areas below stairs or ramps where there is less than 2.1m headroom should either be fully enclosed or be protected by guarding and low-level cane detection, or another form of permanent barrier such as a raised planting bed.

- Bollards should be at least 1000mm in height and contrast visually with background surfaces. A 150mm deep contrasting band is also useful at the top. Adjacent bollards should not be linked with a chain or rope.

- Free-standing posts or columns within access routes should incorporate two visually contrasting bands 1500mm to 1650mm above ground level.

- Cycle parking should be positioned where it will be most useful to cyclists and will not obstruct pedestrians. (The provision of sufficient well-placed cycle stands will reduce ad hoc informal cycle parking which may present a hazard to pedestrians.)

- Cycle parking areas should include space for tandems and adapted cycles. In some locations, weather protection for cycles may be appropriate.

Figure 5.1
**Positioning of street furniture**

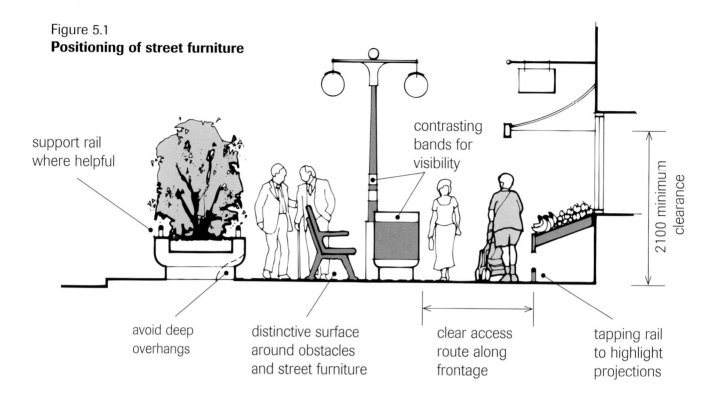

support rail
where helpful

contrasting
bands for
visibility

2100 minimum
clearance

avoid deep
overhangs

distinctive surface
around obstacles
and street furniture

clear access
route along
frontage

tapping rail
to highlight
projections

• Cycle stands should be clearly visible and preferably 1000mm high. Single cycle stands and the ends of Sheffield stands should incorporate a horizontal tapping rail 150mm above ground level.

# 6 External ramps

Where level access cannot be achieved on the approach to a building entrance or across a site, ramps as well as steps should be provided. Ramps enable wheelchair users and people with pushchairs to overcome level changes, but may present difficulties to some ambulant disabled people. Steps should be provided as an alternative except where the change in level is less than 300mm.

- Ramps and steps should be provided where the change in ground level is greater than 300mm. An alternative step-free means of access (an enclosed lift, for example) should be provided if the total rise is greater than 2m.

- In existing buildings where an extreme level change would require a long, circuitous ramp or where space is limited, a short-rise lift may be appropriate (see also *Platform lifts*, page 89) either as an alternative or in addition to the ramp and associated steps.

- Ramped approaches should be clearly signed if not readily apparent.

- The permissible gradient of a ramp is dependent on the length between level landings (the going of the flight). The shallowest possible gradient should be adopted in most circumstances. However, it should be noted that a route with a gradient of 1:20 over a significant distance can still be a potential barrier.

- The maximum permissible gradient is 1:12. See *Figure 6.1* for ramp gradients and corresponding ramp length.

Figure 6.1
**Ramp gradients**

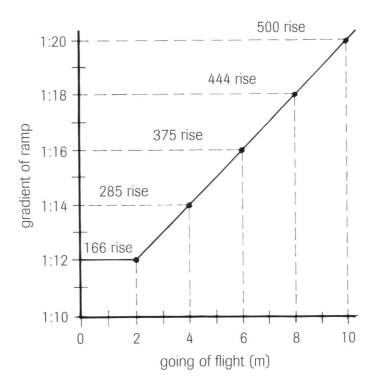

- The total going of a ramp flight should not exceed 10m and the total rise should not exceed 500mm.

- Ramps should be at least 1500mm wide, measured between walls or kerb edgings. A width of 1800mm is preferable in busier locations to enable two wheelchair users to pass each other.

- Where ramps wider than 2.5m are provided, the ramp should be divided using handrails into channels with at least one channel 1.5m wide. The other channels should be between 1m and 2m wide. This will ensure a handrail is within easy reach on either side at all times.

- Ramp flights and landings exposed to the weather should have a gentle cross-fall gradient no greater than 1:50 to ensure rainwater is adequately drained.

- Level unobstructed landings (clear of any door swings) should be provided at the top and bottom of ramps, 1500mm long and the same width as the ramp slope.

Figure 6.2
**Short-rise ramp**

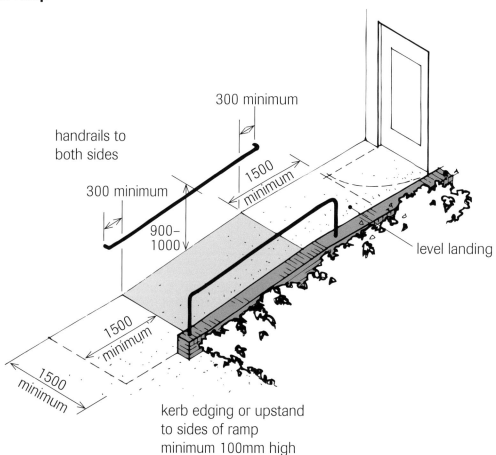

- Intermediate landings should be provided between each ramp slope and be at least 1500mm long (clear of any door swings) where the ramp slopes are in a straight line. Where a change in direction occurs at an intermediate landing, the landing length should be equal to the width of the ramp.

- Intermediate landings at least 1800mm wide and 1800mm long (clear of any door swings) should be provided as passing places on longer ramps or when it is not possible for a wheelchair user to see from one end of the ramp to another.

- Handrails, continuous along each ramp slope and all intermediate landings, should be provided to each side of the ramp, set at appropriate heights and extending beyond the top and bottom of the flight by at least 300mm.

- Edge protection, such as an upstand at least 100mm high, should be provided on the open side of any ramp or landing (in addition to any required guarding or handrail). It should contrast visually with the ramp and landing surface.

Figure 6.3
**Ramp and adjacent steps**

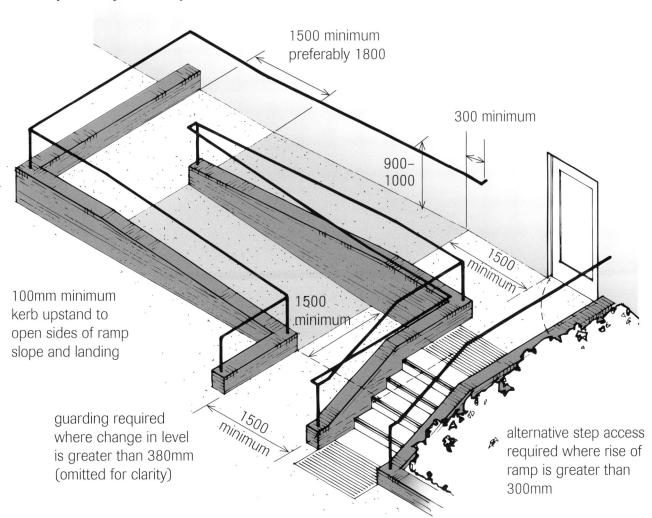

1500 minimum preferably 1800

300 minimum

900–1000

1500 minimum

100mm minimum kerb upstand to open sides of ramp slope and landing

1500 minimum

guarding required where change in level is greater than 380mm (omitted for clarity)

1500 minimum

alternative step access required where rise of ramp is greater than 300mm

- Surface materials should be slip-resistant when wet, firmly fixed, long-lasting and easy to maintain. The ramp surface should contrast visually with the landing surface and edge protection. Patterning which simulates steps, such as applied or inserted slip-resistant strips, should be avoided.

- The frictional characteristics of ramp slopes and landings should be similar, particularly where there is a change of material, to avoid the potential for tripping.

- The slip resistance of surface materials should be carefully considered in conjunction with proposed ramp gradients. Steeper gradients may require a greater slip resistance than shallower gradients and level landings.

- Corduroy hazard warning surfacing should not be used at the top and bottom of ramps as it is not designed for this purpose and causes confusion when used incorrectly.

- Artificial lighting should be provided to the full length of the ramp and all landings and give an even level of illumination of 100 lux (at the surface). Lights should be selected and positioned to avoid creating glare or strong shadows.

## Temporary and portable ramps

- Temporary ramps should meet all the design criteria above. Temporary ramps may be an acceptable solution in situations where building work is underway and access to an existing accessible entrance is not possible, or for short-term facilities such as those provided at a showground.

- Portable ramps should only be used for existing buildings where there is no other option, such as where a stepped doorway is located at the back of a footpath. Portable ramps should be 800mm wide and have upturned edges at least 100mm high. The surface should be slip-resistant and the gradient should be as shallow as possible. Great care should be taken to ensure that portable ramps do not constitute a trip hazard to other people. (Portable ramps consisting of two channels are not suitable as they cannot be used by three-wheeled electrically-powered scooters.)

# 7 External steps

Steps should always be provided as an alternative to ramps where the change in level is greater than 300mm. Although ramps are essential for wheelchair users and people with pushchairs, prams or trolleys, they can present difficulties for other people as a result of the increased travel distance and inclined surface.

Safety for all potential users is critical to the design of steps.

- Single isolated steps should be avoided as these can be difficult to see and present a tripping hazard.

- Stepped routes should be clearly signed if not readily apparent.

- Riser and going dimensions to each step should be consistent within a flight and, wherever possible, between consecutive flights.

- Step risers should be between 150mm and 170mm. Step goings should be between 300mm and 450mm. (Where space is limited adjacent to existing buildings, minor deviations from these measurements may be acceptable.)

- There should be no more than 12 risers in a flight if the treads are less than 350mm, and no more than 18 risers in a flight if the treads are 350mm or more.

- Straight flights of steps are easier to negotiate than curved or dogleg flights. Spiral stairs, tapered treads and tapered risers are not recommended, as they are exceptionally difficult for many people to use.

- The unobstructed width of flights (between walls, balustrades, upstands and strings) should be at least 1200mm. The width between handrails should be at least 1000mm.

Figure 7.1
**Stair dimensions**

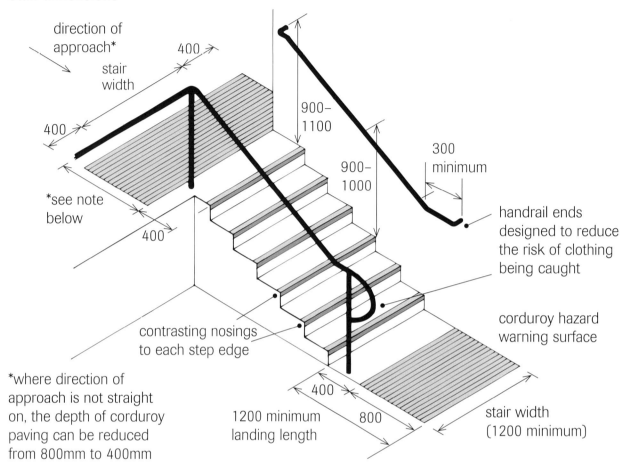

direction of
approach*
stair
width

400

400

900–
1100

900–
1000

300
minimum

*see note
below

400

handrail ends
designed to reduce
the risk of clothing
being caught

corduroy hazard
warning surface

contrasting nosings
to each step edge

*where direction of
approach is not straight
on, the depth of corduroy
paving can be reduced
from 800mm to 400mm

400

1200 minimum
landing length

800

stair width
(1200 minimum)

- A continuous handrail should be provided to both sides of all flights and intermediate landings. Handrails should be provided even where there are only two steps. (See also *Figure 7.1* and *Handrails*, page 46.)

- On flights of steps wider than 2m, handrails should be used to divide the flight into channels to ensure that a handrail is within easy reach on either side. Each channel should be at least 1m wide (between handrails) and no more than 2m wide.

- Level unobstructed landings (clear of any door swings) should be provided at the top and bottom of all flights of steps. The landing length should equal the width of the steps (minimum 1200mm). No doors should open across landings.

- Step flights and landings exposed to the weather should have a gentle cross-fall gradient no greater than 1:50 to ensure rainwater is adequately drained.

- Step treads should be slip-resistant when wet, firmly fixed, long-lasting and easy to maintain. The frictional characteristics of step treads and landings should be similar, particularly where there is a change of material, to avoid the potential for tripping.

- The leading edge of each step should be made apparent with a permanent integral nosing which contrasts visually with the tread and riser surfaces and extends the full width of the step. The nosing should extend 50mm to 65mm horizontally and 30mm to 55mm vertically.

- Projecting step nosings are acceptable if chamfered in profile and limited to a 25mm overlap (see *Figure 7.2*). Perpendicular risers are preferred. Open risers should **not** be used.

- Tactile corduroy hazard warning surfacing, consisting of raised ribs set parallel to the step nosings, should be provided at the top and bottom of each flight as a warning to people with visual impairments of the presence of a change in level (see *Figures 3.4*, page 30 and *7.1*). The position and extent of tactile surfacing is critical to ensure sufficient warning is given about the approaching hazard.

- Corduroy hazard warning surfaces should be used on intermediate landings **only** in specific situations such as where there is an additional access route onto the landing (other than from the steps themselves) or on large intermediate landings where the handrails are not continuous.

- Surface finishes to steps should contrast visually with the landing surfaces.

- Artificial lighting should be provided to the full length of the stair flight and all landings and be positioned to clearly differentiate each step. Lights should be selected and positioned to avoid creating glare or strong shadows and provide an even level of illumination of 100 lux at tread level.

Figure 7.2
**Step profiles**

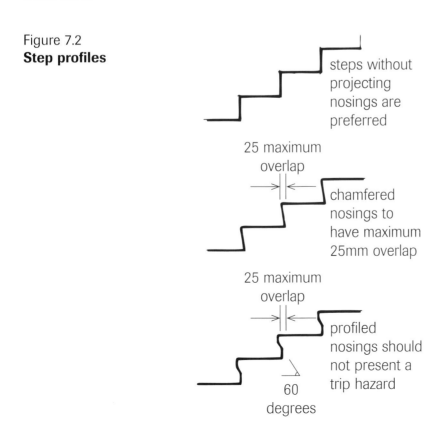

steps without projecting nosings are preferred

25 maximum overlap

chamfered nosings to have maximum 25mm overlap

25 maximum overlap

profiled nosings should not present a trip hazard

60 degrees

# 8 Handrails

Handrails are essential for providing support to people negotiating changes of level, such as ascending and descending ramps, steps and stairs. Handrails are also useful indicators (both tactile and visual) of an approaching change in level, such as at the transition between landing and ramp slope or stair flight. On busy routes, handrails provide reassuring support and directional guidance.

• Handrails should be easy to grip and comfortable to use. Circular and oval profiles are both suitable, with the latter offering better forearm support.

Figure 8.1
**Handrail profiles and dimensions**

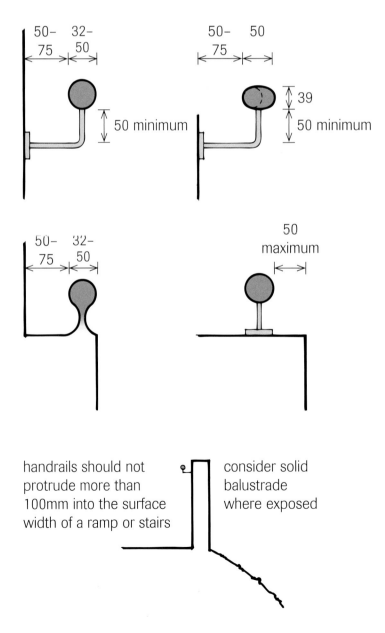

handrails should not protrude more than 100mm into the surface width of a ramp or stairs

consider solid balustrade where exposed

- The height of handrails should be 900mm to 1000mm above the pitch line of ramp slopes and steps and 900mm to 1100mm above landings. See *Figures 6.2* and *6.3*, pages 40 and 41 (in relation to ramps), and *Figure 7.1*, page 44 (in relation to steps).

- Handrails should be continuous along all step flights, ramp slopes and intermediate landings.

- Handrails should extend at least 300mm beyond the top and bottom of a ramp and stair flight to provide support for people as they approach a change in level or pause to rest. It is useful if the handrail turns to the horizontal position to indicate the transition to the corresponding landing area.

- Handrail ends should be carefully considered to reduce the risk of clothing being caught and to ensure they do not project awkwardly into pedestrian routes. A handrail end that gently curves towards the supporting wall or down to the floor is preferred.

- Handrails should be fixed in a manner that enables a person to run their hand along the full length of the rail. (The type and position of handrail supports should not require a person to have to lift their hand off the rail.) The fixings and support structure should be robust enough to support the likely loads imposed on it.

- The provision of a second (lower) handrail for use by children and people of short stature is recommended for buildings accessible to the general public and buildings predominantly used by children. The second handrail should be positioned 600mm above the pitchline of the steps or ramp slope. (In some cases, additional guarding may be required above the upper handrail to prevent a child falling if they climbed onto the lower handrail.)

- Surfaces such as hardwood or nylon-coated steel are recommended in preference to surface materials that are cold to the touch. Materials that are susceptible to significant changes in temperature due to their location should be avoided, such as stainless steel.

- Handrails should contrast visually with the surface they are viewed against. Highly reflective surfaces should be avoided.

- Balustrades, in particular to ramps and landings, should be sufficiently robust to withstand impact from powered wheelchairs and scooters.

# Internal environment

## 9 Entrances

In new buildings, the principal entrance (or entrances) should be accessible to everyone. In existing buildings, where it is not possible for the main entrance (or entrances) to be accessible, consideration should be given to relocating the main entrance. Alternatively, an additional entrance should be provided which is accessible for all potential users.

### Identification, signage and approach

- Entrances to buildings should be placed in a logical relationship with the route of approach and be easily distinguishable from the façade.

- Entrance doors should contrast visually with surrounding surfaces.

- Alternative accessible entrances should be signposted both from the edge of the site and from the main entrance. Signs should incorporate the International Symbol for Access.

- Clear signs indicating the location of the entrance should be provided and be visible from all approaches to the building.

Figure 9.1
**Entrance identification**

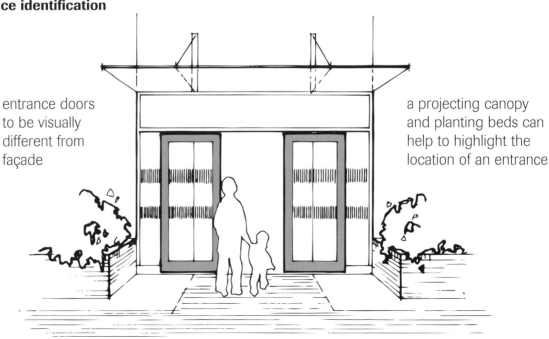

entrance doors to be visually different from façade

a projecting canopy and planting beds can help to highlight the location of an entrance

approach routes to be logically arranged in relation to entrance doors

- The area immediately in front of the accessible entrance (at least 1500mm × 1500mm) should be level and have a surface which does not impede wheelchairs. Structural supports should be clearly identifiable so that they do not present a hazard for visually impaired people.

- Canopies over entrances (or recessed entrance doors) should be considered as a means of providing protection from bad weather, particularly at entrances with manual doors or entry systems.

- Columns supporting entrance canopies should be positioned away from pedestrian access routes so as not to cause an obstruction or hazard.

- Outward-opening doors should be protected or recessed (see *Figure 9.2*).

- Revolving doors, including those with a very large diameter, are not considered accessible. If they are used, they should always be supplemented with a fully operational adjacent swing door which should always be available for use.

Figure 9.2
**Outward-opening doors**

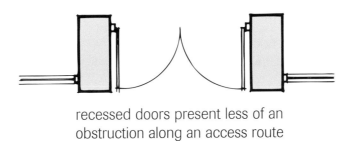

recessed doors present less of an
obstruction along an access route

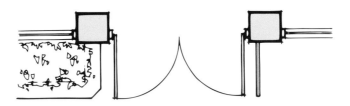

planting beds and guardrails can be used to
protect pedestrians from outward-opening doors

## Threshold and surfaces

- Door thresholds should be flush wherever possible. A maximum overall change in level of 15mm is permissible for external entrance doors, if required, for weather protection. Wherever possible, the profile of the threshold should comprise a gradual slope and / or minimal upstands. Any upstand more than 5mm should be chamfered or pencil-rounded, as in *Figure 9.3*.

- Drainage gratings and channels adjacent to door thresholds should be flush with adjacent paving surfaces.

- Thresholds to internal doors should be flush with the floor finish on both sides of the door. Junctions and edges of all floor finishes should be firmly fixed.

- External surface materials and internal floor finishes should be neatly laid flush with the door threshold and firmly secured so as not to present a trip hazard.

- Entrance matting, designed to remove dirt and moisture from footwear and wheels, should extend from the external entrance door at least 1500mm into the building. A larger area of matting is likely to be required for busy entrances.

- Loose-laid entrance mats are best avoided as these can creep across the floor and often become curled along the edge, presenting a trip hazard to all users.

- The junction between all floor finishes, such as between the entrance matting and adjacent surface, should be flush. All edges should be firmly fixed to avoid potential trip hazards.

- Coir matting and other compressible materials should be avoided as they can be difficult for wheelchair users to travel across as well as for pushchairs and trolleys.

Figure 9.3
**Door threshold profile**

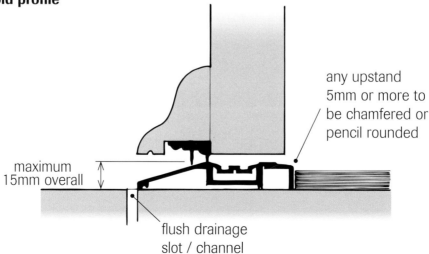

any upstand 5mm or more to be chamfered or pencil rounded

maximum 15mm overall

flush drainage slot / channel

## Entrance lobbies

• Lobbies should be sized to provide convenient access for all and enable people to move clear of the first set of doors before opening the second.

• Double leaf doors arranged for straight through travel are recommended for entrance lobbies. The depth of the lobby should equal 1570mm plus the projection of any door swing opening into the lobby.

• Double swing doors should be used for lobbies wherever possible as they offer travel in both directions.

• Where lobbies with single leaf doors are required, the lobby arrangement should be as shown in *Figure 9.4* (overleaf).

• Where lobbies have automatic sliding doors or reduced swing doors, the length of the lobby may be reduced as less space is needed to manoeuvre around door swings.

• Artificial lighting to entrance lobbies should provide as gradual a transition as possible between the exterior and interior environment.

• Glazing within the lobby should not create distracting reflections. Full-height glazing should have manifestation markings to ensure it is clearly visible. (See also *Glazed doors*, page 57.)

• Projections such as columns, ducts or fixtures should not project into the access route within a lobby by more than 100mm. Where unavoidable, projections greater than this should be guarded and contrast visually with adjacent surfaces.

Figure 9.4
**Lobby dimensions**

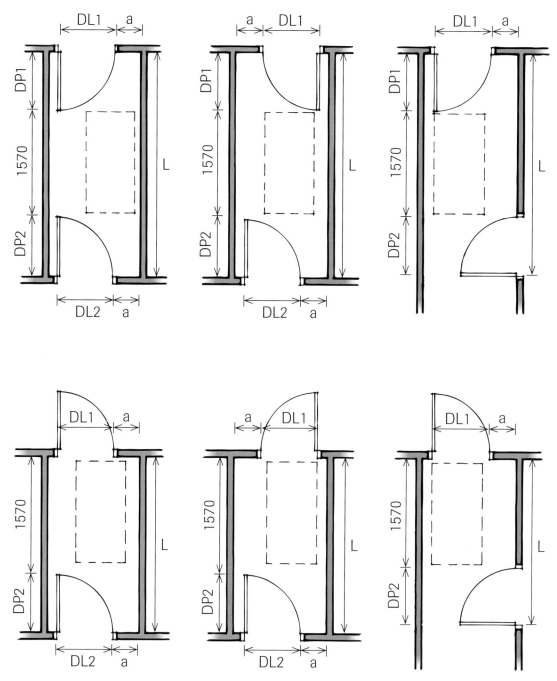

DL1 and DL2 = door leaf dimensions of lobby doors
DP1 and DP2 = door projection into lobby
L = Minimum lobby length, or length up to door leaf for side entry lobby
a = Minimum 300mm clear space (can be increased to reduce L)

1570mm long space represents area for wheelchair user and assistant

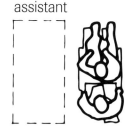

# 10 Doors – external and internal

## Door dimensions

- The minimum effective clear width of external entrance doors, inner lobby doors and internal doors is shown in *Table 10.1*.

**Table 10.1**
**Minimum effective clear widths of doors**

| Types of doors | | Minimum effective clear width | |
| --- | --- | --- | --- |
| | | **New buildings** | **Existing buildings** |
| Entrance doors to all buildings accessed by the general public (includes external doors and inner lobby doors) | | 1000mm | 775mm |
| All other doors where the direction of approach is: | straight on | 800mm | 750mm |
| | • at right angles from route 1500mm wide | 800mm | 750mm |
| | • at right angles from route 1200mm wide | 825mm | 775mm |
| | • at right angles from route 900mm wide | Not appropriate | 800mm |

- Effective clear width should be measured from the face of the door when open (or any projecting door handles) to the opposite frame or doorstop, as in *Figure 10.1*.

Figure 10.1
**Measuring effective clear widths of doors**

door open at 90 degrees

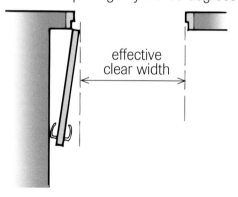

door opening less than 90 degrees

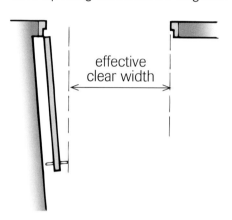

door opening beyond 90 degrees

sliding door

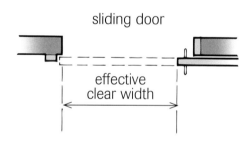

• A clear space at least 300mm wide (450mm preferred) should be available adjacent to the opening edge of a door to enable easy access to the door handle and to allow convenient manoeuvre around the door as it opens. See *Figure 10.2*.

Figure 10.2
**Clear manoeuvring space**

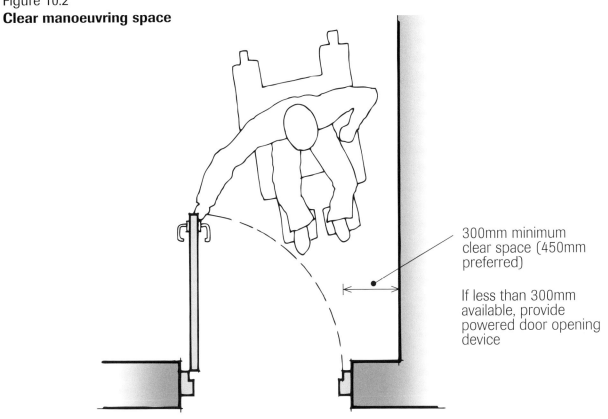

300mm minimum
clear space (450mm
preferred)

If less than 300mm
available, provide
powered door opening
device

• In existing buildings where there is less than 300mm clear space adjacent to the opening edge of a door, a power-operated door opening system should be provided with either manual or automatic activation, as appropriate (see *Doors – opening and closing systems*, page 60).

# Vision panels

- External entrance doors and entrance lobby doors should have vision panels to enable people to see and be seen through the doors in both directions.

- Internal doors across corridors and to internal lobbies and doors which form part of an emergency escape route should also have vision panels.

- Where doors comprise a main door leaf and openable side panel (often termed leaf-and-a-half doors), the side panel should have a vision panel if it is wider than 450mm, as well as the main door leaf.

- Vision panels should provide a zone of visibility between 500mm and 1500mm above floor level, but can extend lower and higher than this, as in *Figure 10.3*.

- If two or more smaller vision panels are provided to a door leaf, the zone of visibility should not be reduced in height by more than a total of 350mm. Where the zone of visibility is interrupted, a vision panel should be located at the top and bottom of the zone.

- Vision panels may be positioned centrally or towards the opening edge of the door leaf and should be at least 100mm wide.

Figure 10.3
**Door vision panels**

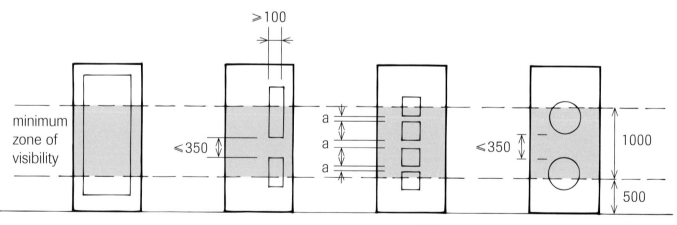

a+a+a≤350mm

- It is justifiable in some specific circumstances, such as for reasons of security or privacy, for vision panels to be smaller than otherwise required or omitted altogether.

## Glazed doors

- Substantially glazed doors and side panels should have permanent manifestation markings for safety and visibility which should be at two heights, between 850mm and 1000mm, and between 1400mm and 1600mm.

Figure 10.4
**Markings for safety and visibility**

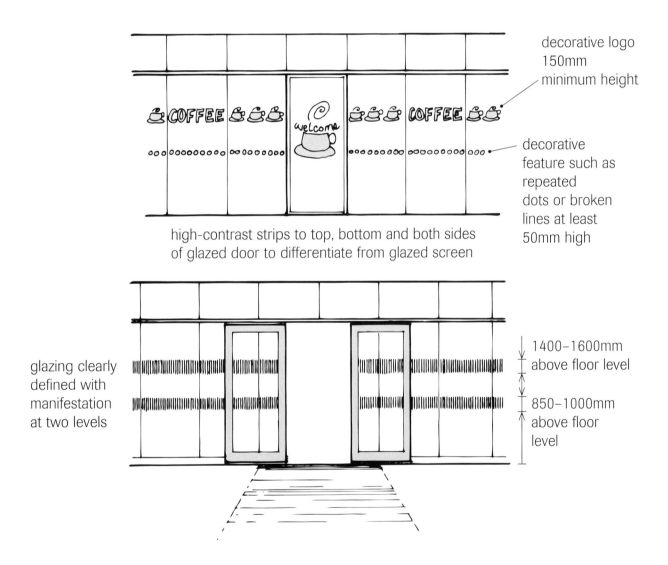

decorative logo 150mm minimum height

decorative feature such as repeated dots or broken lines at least 50mm high

high-contrast strips to top, bottom and both sides of glazed door to differentiate from glazed screen

COFFEE welcome COFFEE

glazing clearly defined with manifestation at two levels

1400–1600mm above floor level

850–1000mm above floor level

- Manifestation markings should contrast visually with the surfaces they are viewed against and be clearly visible in all light conditions. Two-tone markings are recommended to improve visibility.

- It is helpful if the markings to a glazed door differ from those of an adjacent glazed screen in order to highlight the location of the door.

- Markings comprising a repeated logo or pattern at least 150mm high or a 50mm high continuous band are recommended.

- Where the door is located adjacent to a glazed screen, the top edge and both sides of glass doors should be clearly differentiated by highly contrasting strips.

- Fully glazed, frameless entrance doors are not recommended. If used, and where capable of being held open, they should be protected by guarding to prevent the leading edge constituting a hazard.

- Fully glazed doors are not recommended along corridors.

## Door markings

- The leading edge of doors that are to be held open, and of outward-opening doors along internal access routes, should contrast visually with the door face. This can be achieved by either

  - a 15mm wide intumescent strip to the full height of the door, contrasting visually with the door material, or

  - a self-adhesive strip extending from 500mm to 1500mm above floor level and covering at least 60 per cent of the door edge.

# 11 Doors – access control systems

Access and entry systems are commonly used to control access to building entrances and to areas within buildings such as to particular departments or staff-only facilities. Entry systems linked to powered door-opening devices are particularly beneficial in that doors are activated to open when entry is permitted. Although provided to control access, the design and position of entry systems and other systems should not present difficulties to anyone needing to use them.

## Entry systems

• Entry system controls should be positioned adjacent to the leading edge of the door, within 200mm of the door opening and between 900mm and 1100mm high.

• The approach to door entry controls should be clear of obstructions, level and positioned away from any projecting columns or return walls.

• All entry systems should contrast visually with the surface they are mounted on and be well lit.

## Entryphones

• Door entryphones should facilitate both audible and visual communication, such as in the form of a video entryphone. They should include visual and audible acknowledgement that the call has been received and the door lock released.

• Entryphones should include an LED text display capable of duplicating audible information such as 'Speak now' and 'Please enter'.

• Entryphones should be simple to use, with call buttons easy to identify using clear tactile symbols and effective visual contrast.

## Security devices

• Security systems that require the use of an electronically programmed card or fob should be easy for all to use. Proximity card or fob systems are preferred to swipe card systems.

• Swipe card systems, where used, should be positioned vertically at a preferred height of between 950mm and 1000mm above floor level (although 900mm to 1100mm is acceptable).

## Turnstiles

Where turnstiles or ticket-control barriers are provided, at least one hinged gate should be provided in addition which should be at least 800mm wide and suitable for a wheelchair at least 1200mm long. (Refer also to *Accessible Train Station Design for Disabled People: A Code of Practice*).

# 12 Doors – opening and closing systems

The design and selection of door furniture, mechanical self-closing devices and any electrically-powered device or operating system can have a significant effect on the accessibility of doors, whether external or internal. Door handles that are difficult to grip or poorly-adjusted mechanical self-closing devices can present an immediate barrier to access, as can entry systems that rely only on audible communication or are positioned out of reach.

All door characteristics such as size, weight, style, position and function (security and / or fire resistance) should be fully considered when selecting appropriate door furniture and when specifying the use of entry systems and powered-opening devices.

## Door furniture

- Door handles to manually-operated doors with a latch should be lever handles (*Figure 12.1*) and be capable of being used with one hand without the need to grip or twist the handle.

- D-pull handles are suitable for doors without a latch and are recommended to be positioned on the pull side of a door only.

- The size and position of door handles is shown in *Figure 12.3*, page 62.

- Horizontal grabrails should be provided to outward-opening doors such as accessible WC doors, to enable people to close the door behind them. The preferred fixing height is 900mm (although 800mm to 1050mm is acceptable). As the grabrails can reduce the effective clear door opening width, additional door width should be provided.

- All door opening furniture should contrast visually with the door.

- Hinges should be selected to suit the mass of the door and potential additional loading such as a person leaning on the door or handles for support. Low-friction hinges resist wear and reduce opening and closing forces.

- Swing-clear hinges may be useful in existing buildings in order to maximise the effective clear opening width. (When the door is open, these hinges align the edge of the door with the door stop, thereby increasing the width of the opening.)

- Pivot hinges, when used in conjunction with an emergency release bolt, are useful for doors that are usually inward-opening, but which may be required to open outwards in an emergency, such as doors to a bathroom.

Figure 12.1
**Door lever handle details**

Figure 12.2
**D-pull handles**

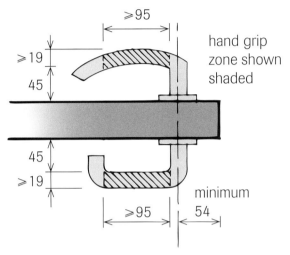

lever handle profiles returned towards door leaf, for
solid doors and doors with wider stiles (≥100mm)

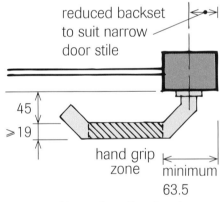

profiled lever handles for doors
with narrower stiles (<100mm)

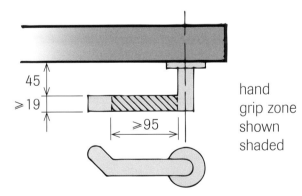

cranked lever handles for solid doors and
doors with wider stiles (≥100mm)

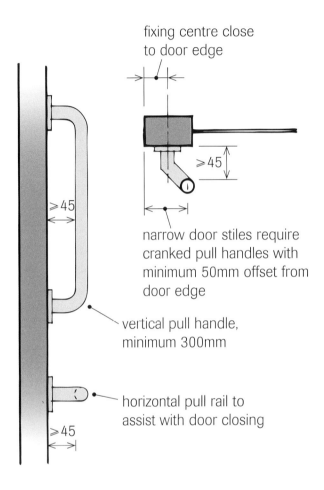

fixing centre close
to door edge

narrow door stiles require
cranked pull handles with
minimum 50mm offset from
door edge

vertical pull handle,
minimum 300mm

horizontal pull rail to
assist with door closing

- Latched doors which are fitted with a self-closing device should have a modified strike plate with a gravity cam as this reduces latch resistance and therefore also reduces the force required to close the door fully.

- Keyways to locks should either be positioned above the lever handle in order to be clearly visible and easy to operate or, if positioned below, be at least 72mm clear of the handle.

- Where turns or snibs are used to operate locks, they should be suitable for people with limited manual dexterity and incorporate larger winged-turns or levers where possible.

- Door bolts, if required, should be easy to use and be one of the following:

  – a lever-action flush bolt

  – a slide-action flush bolt with an easy-grip knob

  – an espagnolette bolt (incorporating top and bottom shoot bars) operated by a single-lever handle positioned between 900mm and 1050mm above floor level

  – a rack and pinion mortise bolt with a permanent easy-grip knob / handle.

Figure 12.3
**Heights of door handles**

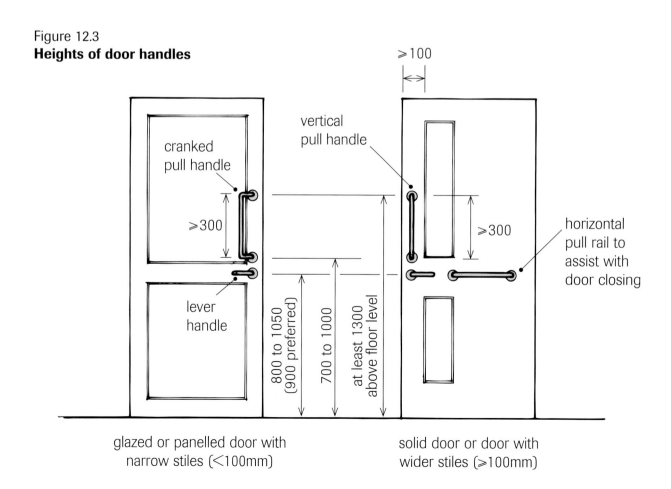

glazed or panelled door with
narrow stiles (<100mm)

solid door or door with
wider stiles (≥100mm)

- Emergency exit devices should be capable of being released with a force no greater than:

  – 80 Newton for horizontal push bar panic exit devices

  – 70 Newton for lever handle emergency exit devices

  – 150 Newton for push pad emergency exit devices.

## Door self-closing devices

Doors fitted with mechanical self-closing devices for fire safety, privacy, security or environmental reasons can be difficult for people to open due to the force required to overcome the closing pressure. Some devices close very quickly when the door is released and this too can create difficulties for people who may be slow moving.

- Self-closing devices should be carefully matched with the size and weight of the door and take account of the effect of air pressure, door / frame seals, hinge friction and latch resistance.

- High-efficiency self-closing devices should be used in preference to low-efficiency devices as they are able to operate effectively using a reduced opening force.

- The force required to open a door fitted with a self-closing device should be no greater than 30 Newton (from the closed position up to 30 degrees of opening) and no greater than 22.5 Newton (from 30 to 60 degrees of opening).

- The maximum force exerted by the self-closing device as it closes the door should be within zero and 15 degrees.

- Consider the need for a delayed-action facility to ensure the door remains open long enough for people who are slow moving. (Delayed-action is not suitable for doors on circulation routes.)

- Self-closing devices should be site-adjustable (both speed and force) and regularly maintained to ensure they are working efficiently at all times.

- Any backcheck facility should not reduce the effective clear opening width of the door.

- Self-closing devices should be avoided where there is no mandatory or particular reason for their use. The overuse of door closers presents an unnecessary barrier to all building users.

# Door hold-open devices

The presence of a series of doors along a circulation route, all fitted with self-closing devices for fire safety reasons, is likely to impede access for many building users. In some situations, the size and other characteristics of individual doors will mean the forces required to open the door exceed the recommended limits (see above). In other cases, it may simply be preferable for a door to be held open for ease of access.

In buildings with a fully automatic fire detection and alarm system, the use of electrically-powered hold-open devices or swing-free devices can greatly improve accessibility in a range of circumstances.

- Swing-free hold-open devices are suitable for inward-opening room doors, but should be avoided for doors on circulation routes.

- Electromagnetic hold-open devices are suitable for doors on circulation routes.

- Electromagnetic hold-open devices should be capable of being released manually such as by using a push button. The button should be easy to identify and accessible.

- Consider any electromagnetic hold-open devices that are placed along evacuation routes. These should release upon fire alarm evacuation and may create barriers along escape routes. Appropriate management of suitable routes and plans should be devised (see also *Means of escape*, page 129).

- Regular tests should be undertaken to ensure all hold-open devices are fail-safe in the event of a power failure.

# Power-operated doors

Power-operated door opening and closing systems overcome many of the difficulties associated with the weight of manually-operated doors. They are especially useful for main entrance doors which may otherwise require powerful closing mechanisms to hold doors shut in strong winds and to counteract differences in pressure between the internal and external environment.

Selection of the most appropriate type of power-operation and activation device together with appropriate positioning and safety systems will ensure ease of use and adequate warning for all building users.

- The approach to power-operated doors should be direct, clear and level. Power-operated doors should not be positioned at the top or bottom of ramps or sloping floors.

- Power-operated swing doors should not open across any adjacent access route.

- Fully automatic doors, activated by a presence and motion detector, offer easy access for everyone and are the preferred arrangement where access to buildings is freely available.

- Where access is required to be controlled, the use of a security device such as a hands-free proximity reader could be used to activate the door opening mechanism.

- Automatic doors should open early enough and stay open long enough to allow safe entry and exit, particularly for people who move slowly. The sensor should be set to activate the door so that it is fully open when the person approaching is no closer than 1400mm.

- Automatic doors that open towards people should have clear Automatic Door markings and indicate the direction of opening.

- In situations in which fully automatic doors are not suitable, such as where the movement of passing pedestrians may inadvertently activate the door opening mechanism to an entrance, the use of manually-activated controls should be considered.

- Selection of controls for manually-activated doors should consider the needs of all potential building users and any security requirements. Controls may comprise a wall-mounted push pad, swipe card or hand-held remote control.

- Manual controls – push pads, card swipes, proximity readers or coded entry – for powered doors should be located between 750mm and 1000mm above floor level, as shown in *Figure 12.4*. On the opening side of the door, the controls should be set back 1400mm from the leading edge so that the person using the controls does not have to move to avoid contact with the door as it opens. The controls should be clearly distinguishable from the background.

- Key pads should be large and easy to operate with tactile identification.

- All power-operated doors should have both presence and motion detectors for safety.

- All power-operated doors should be capable of being operated manually in the event of a power failure.

Figure 12.4
**Position of manual activation system**

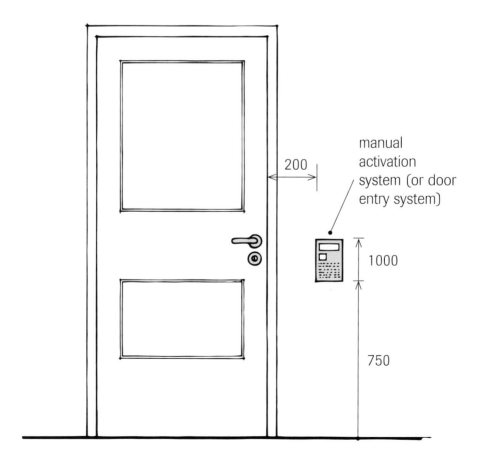

# 13 Entrance foyers

A well-designed entrance foyer enables people to make a comfortable and gentle transition between the external and internal environment and to orientate themselves within a building. The design of entrance foyers should help to make people feel welcome within a building as well as empowered to locate the facilities or services they require.

Figure 13.1
**Entrance foyers**

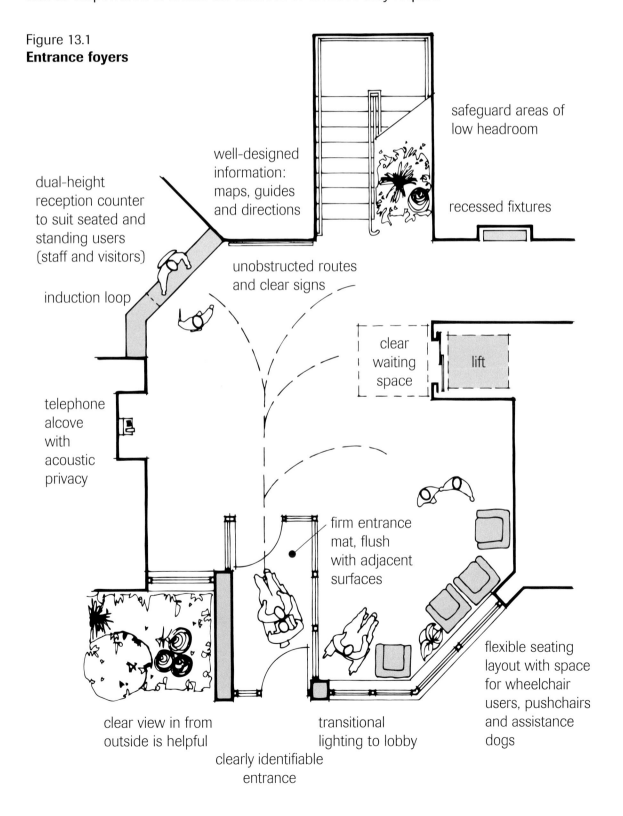

dual-height reception counter to suit seated and standing users (staff and visitors)

induction loop

well-designed information: maps, guides and directions

safeguard areas of low headroom

recessed fixtures

unobstructed routes and clear signs

clear waiting space

lift

telephone alcove with acoustic privacy

firm entrance mat, flush with adjacent surfaces

flexible seating layout with space for wheelchair users, pushchairs and assistance dogs

clear view in from outside is helpful

transitional lighting to lobby

clearly identifiable entrance

## Layout and orientation

• Foyers should be logically arranged and have plenty of space for general circulation.

• Routes to reception areas, lifts, stairs and WCs should be easy to identify and unobstructed.

• Reception desks should be easy to identify and be accessed via a direct route from the entrance. (If external noise levels are high and likely to affect communications, the reception desk should not be located too close to the doors.)

• Signs to key facilities such as lifts, stairs, WCs and reception / information desks should be obvious, clear and easy to understand. Where relevant, signs to other parts of the building and to principal circulation routes should also be provided.

• Signs should include pictograms and universally recognised symbols as well as plain English and incorporate tactile as well as visual information. (See also *Wayfinding, information and signs*, page 108.)

• Seating should be provided within entrance foyers and in conjunction with reception desks. (See also *Seating*, page 73.)

## Surface finishes

• Floor finishes within entrance foyers should be firm, smooth and slip-resistant.

• Junctions between different materials should be flush and all edges should be firmly fixed to avoid potential trip hazards.

• Surface finishes can be used creatively to highlight circulation routes and delineate other areas such as seating or waiting areas. (See also *Surfaces*, page 80.)

## Queuing barriers and rails

• Where permanent or temporary queuing barriers are required, such as within the entrance foyer of large visitor attractions, they should be positioned and spaced to enable easy access for everyone.

• The distance between the reception / service desk and queuing barrier or rail should be at least 1800mm if there is a knee recess to the desk or 2200mm where there is no knee recess.

• Queuing barriers and rails should contrast visually with surrounding surfaces.

• Permanent barriers should have a rigid top and bottom rail. The top rail should be strong enough for people to lean on to rest and the bottom rail designed as a tapping rail, with the lower edge no more than 150mm above floor level.

• The bases of queuing barrier posts should not present a potential trip hazard or reduce the available width of the queuing channel.

# 14 Reception desks and service counters

Reception desks typically provide the first point of contact between staff and visitors close to the entrance of a building. Service counters are typically provided where transactions are undertaken, such as in a ticket office or a payment counter in a shop. All such counters and desks should be designed to be accessed and used – on both staff and customer sides – by as wide a range of people as possible.

## Location and approach

• Reception desks should be positioned away from potential sources of noise (both internal or external), such as café seating areas, external doors and openable windows.

• Avoid positioning counters and desks in front of windows where bright sunshine may cause a person's face to be silhouetted as this makes it difficult to lip-read and follow sign language. Backgrounds with strong patterns or reflective surfaces should also be avoided.

• Clear manoeuvring space should be provided to both the staff and customer side (*Figure 14.1*). Approach to the counter or desk on both sides should be direct and unobstructed.

Figure 14.1
**Manoeuvring space to reception counters / service desks**

Clear manoeuvring space:
A: Counter / desktop without knee recess
B: Counter / desktop with knee recess

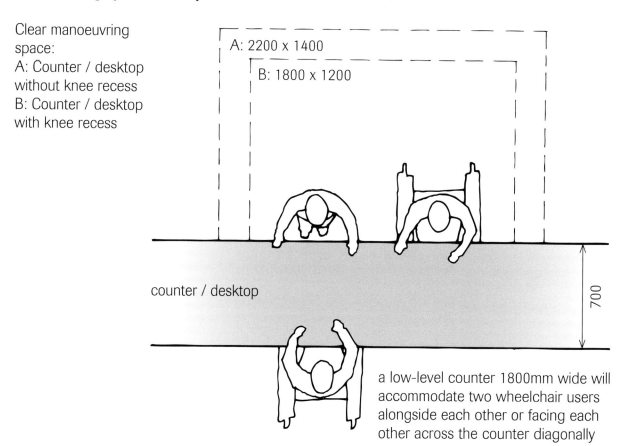

A: 2200 x 1400

B: 1800 x 1200

counter / desktop

700

a low-level counter 1800mm wide will accommodate two wheelchair users alongside each other or facing each other across the counter diagonally

• Consider providing a quiet area or interview room nearby for customers who need minimal background noise and distraction in order to communicate effectively. Such a room is also useful for people requiring confidentiality.

• The floor level should be the same on both the staff and customer sides in most circumstances.

• In venues where it is preferable for staff to be positioned higher than customers, a ramp with a gradient no steeper than 1:12 should be provided to the raised area.

## Detail and surfaces

• Counters and desks should be set at two heights:

   – 760mm high for people seated and with a knee recess at least 700mm high

   – between 950mm and 1100mm for people standing. If there is sufficient space, two higher counters may be provided, one 950mm high and one 1100mm high. (This is in addition to the lower counter for seated approach.)

Figure 14.2
**Reception / service desk dimensions**

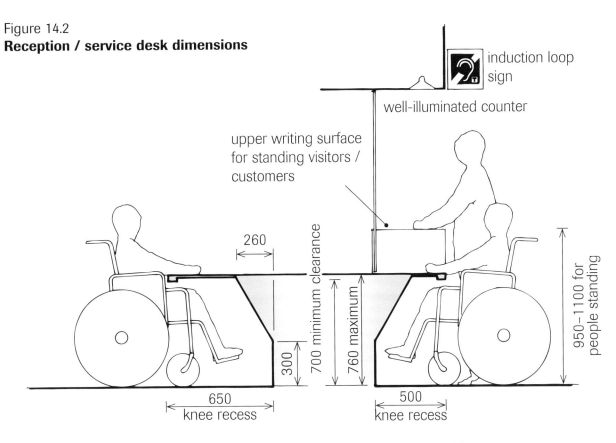

**Staff / receptionist side**
The desk dimensions enable a member of staff using a wheelchair with desk armrests to sit close to a counter at normal desk height.

**Visitor / customer side**
The dimensions enable a visitor using a wheelchair to bring the arms of their wheelchair to the edge of the counter in order to read and sign papers.

**71**

- Knee recesses should be 500mm deep on the customer side and 650mm deep on the staff side. The deeper recess enables staff who are wheelchair users to sit closer to the counter.

- The counter depth where there is space for a wheelchair user (on either the staff or customer side) should be at least 700mm.

- The lower section of counters should be at least 1500mm wide, although 1800mm is preferred.

- An upward-sloping profile should be considered for the leading edge of counters where people are required to pick up coins or tickets. This can assist people with limited dexterity.

- Visual contrast between the counter surface, edgings and adjacent floor and wall surfaces is recommended.

- All exposed edges and corners should be well rounded.

## Communication

- Where sliding glass windows are installed they should be fully openable so as not to impede conversation.

- Where fixed glazed screens are required for security purposes, a voice amplification system should be provided.

- A counter induction loop should be provided where it can be used by staff and customers. The induction loop should be clearly signed and available for use at all times.

- Where several positions are available for customer service, such as in a large ticket office, induction loops should be spaced far enough apart to avoid overspill. (See also *Hearing enhancement systems*, page 115.)

- Artificial lighting should be carefully designed to ensure that the staff / receptionist's face and the customer's face are clearly visible to allow lip-reading.

- Provision of seats near low counters could be considered.

- Ensure the acoustics within staff areas and reception, particularly if they are busy, do not create echo or unnecessary reverberation.

# 15 Seating

The provision of seating to enable people to rest or wait greatly improves the accessibility of buildings and external areas. Seats placed at intervals along paths or within large buildings provide a place to rest but can also be an amenity itself such as to enjoy a view in a park or to observe events in an exhibition hall.

## Provision and layout

• Seats should be provided at intervals along long routes (externally and internally) and where waiting is likely. (See *Pedestrian routes*, page 25; *Horizontal circulation*, page 76; and *Entrance foyers*, page 67.)

• Seats should be set back from pedestrian routes so they do not obstruct or narrow the circulation width.

• Access to seating should be direct and unobstructed.

• All seating should be positioned on a level ground or floor surface.

• A clear space (preferably 1.5m × 1.5m) should be provided to the side of fixed seats, such as seats in a park, to enable a wheelchair user to sit alongside a companion, or for a pushchair or an assistance dog.

• Where rows of seats are provided, such as in waiting rooms, a clear space at least 900mm wide × 1400mm deep should be provided for wheelchair users in addition to space for manoeuvring, as shown in *Figure 15.1*, page 74. Space should be provided to enable two wheelchair users to sit alongside each other or for a wheelchair user to sit alongside a companion in a fixed seat.

• A clear width of 1200mm should be maintained to a proportion of the cross-aisles to enable easy access for people who need more space.

• A clear space, equivalent in size to a standard seat, within or at the end of a row in a block of seating should be provided for an assistance dog, clear of the aisles.

## Seating style

- Seats in external areas should be provided in a range of heights between 380mm and 580mm. A height of 480mm is considered suitable for wheelchair users. Fixed seating within buildings should have a compressed cushion height between 450mm and 475mm.

- Seats with armrests should be provided to assist people when lowering themselves onto the seat and raising themselves to stand.

Figure 15.1
**General seating layouts**

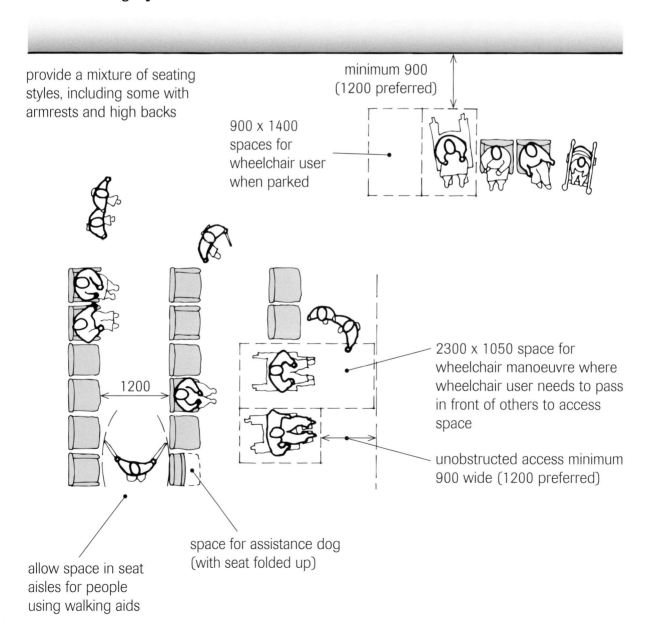

provide a mixture of seating styles, including some with armrests and high backs

900 x 1400 spaces for wheelchair user when parked

minimum 900 (1200 preferred)

1200

2300 x 1050 space for wheelchair manoeuvre where wheelchair user needs to pass in front of others to access space

unobstructed access minimum 900 wide (1200 preferred)

allow space in seat aisles for people using walking aids

space for assistance dog (with seat folded up)

- Some seating positions on rows of fixed seating should allow for wheelchair users to transfer out of their wheelchair and onto the seat. These seats should not have an armrest at the end of the row as this will prevent lateral transfer. The armrest should be set in away from the end of the row.

- Seats with backs should always be available. Where fixed bench-style seating is provided seat backs should be provided to at least half of the seating positions.

- Wherever possible, seats within buildings should have cushions.

- Some seats that are wider and higher than standard should be provided for people of large stature.

- Seats should not be mounted on a plinth.

- In some circumstances, the availability of a range of fixed and loose seating offers flexibility in the use of space.

- In larger buildings where a lot of seating is provided, or in areas where waiting times are short, consider the provision of perch seats (fixed or fold-down) at a height of 650mm to 800mm.

- Seating should visually contrast with surrounding surfaces.

  For detailed guidance on audience and spectator seating, see BS 8300 and Sport England's *Accessible Sports Facilities.*

# 16 Horizontal circulation

Circulation routes such as corridors, passageways, lobbies and aisles all provide access to and emergency exit from buildings and should be independently accessible to everyone. Circulation routes should be simple and safe to negotiate. If logically arranged, well lit and with appropriate surface finishes, they also aid navigation and help people to orientate themselves within a building.

## Corridors and passageways

• Consideration should be given to the anticipated numbers of people and expected patterns of use when designing circulation routes. Increased widths should be provided where necessary.

• Circulation routes should be logical and reasonably direct. Where appropriate, corridor layouts should be replicated at each floor level.

• Corridors and passageways should be unobstructed as far as possible. Items such as radiators and fire extinguishers should be recessed. Where unavoidable, obstructions should be easy to identify and protected with a guardrail.

• Wherever practical, a clear width of 1800mm is recommended to enable people to pass each other comfortably and to turn through 180 degrees.

• Where routes are less than 1800mm wide, regular passing places should be provided 1800mm wide × 1800mm long. Turning areas should be provided at junctions to enable people to change direction or turn and return along a route. Splayed or rounded corners at junctions are beneficial.

• Internal circulation routes should have a minimum clear width of 1200mm.

• In existing buildings, where there is a narrowing of the route over a short distance due to a permanent obstruction, the clear width should not be less than 1000mm. (This is unlikely to be permitted if the route is an emergency exit route.)

• Outward-opening doors in frequently used corridors should be recessed.

• Outward-opening doors, such as doors to accessible WCs, may be acceptable if the corridor is 1800mm wide, if the corridor is used infrequently and is not an emergency exit route. The corridor floor must also be level outside the door.

• Along corridors and emergency escape routes, where there is a series of double doors with one leaf wider than the other (leaf-and-a-half doors), the wider leaf should be on the same side over the length of the corridor.

Figure 16.1
**Corridor dimensions**

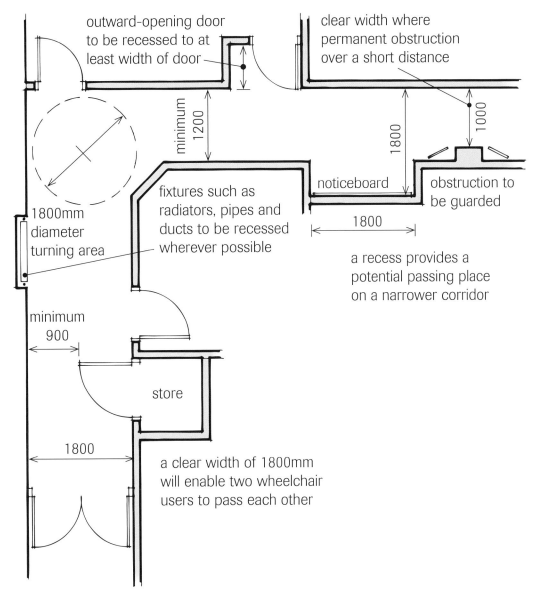

outward-opening door
to be recessed to at
least width of door

clear width where
permanent obstruction
over a short distance

minimum 1200

1800

1000

1800mm diameter turning area

fixtures such as radiators, pipes and ducts to be recessed wherever possible

noticeboard

obstruction to be guarded

1800

a recess provides a potential passing place on a narrower corridor

minimum 900

store

1800

a clear width of 1800mm will enable two wheelchair users to pass each other

- It is beneficial if the doors along access routes are double swing so that they can be pushed open in both directions.

- In existing buildings where corridor widths are narrower than recommended, it is helpful for doors into adjoining areas to be wider to enable people to turn comfortably through the doorway.

- In sports buildings where the use of sports wheelchairs (typically 1200mm wide) is proposed, a sports chair zone should be incorporated into the design. The sports chair zone should comprise wider doors, lobbies and circulation areas sufficient to enable convenient access and manoeuvre between the entrance / reception, activity area, wheelchair storage and emergency exits. Refer to *Accessible Sports Facilities* for detailed guidance.

## Open-plan areas

• In open-plan areas such as offices and retail showrooms, circulation route widths should follow the guidance for corridors and passageways above.

• Consider defining circulation routes with visually contrasting floor finishes and textures.

• Artificial lighting can be used to help highlight circulation routes.

• Alterations to the furniture layout and displays should not compromise circulation routes.

## Aisles to fixed storage

• Access to fixed storage in workplaces and areas of buildings used by the public should be as accessible as possible. At least one unit should be fully accessible.

• Access to storage areas should be as direct as possible and unobstructed. The location should be readily apparent or clearly signed.

• Some storage with knee recesses and an aisle width of 1200mm should be provided, where possible, to enable frontal approach.

• Where there is no knee recess, the aisle width should be at least 1400mm.

## Internal lobbies

For recommended internal lobby layouts, see *Figure 9.4*, page 52.

## Changes in level

• In new buildings, internal circulation routes should be level. Where changes of level are unavoidable, such as in existing buildings, the route may be gently inclined. For routes with a gradient between 1:60 and 1:20, the sloped surface should be clearly differentiated and there should be a level rest area at least 1500mm long for every 500mm rise in level.

• Any sections within a corridor steeper than 1:20 should be designed as an internal ramp (see also *Internal ramps, steps, stairs and handrails*, page 83). Where the change in level is 300mm or greater, steps should be provided in addition to a ramp.

• Where a section of corridor is divided (for example between a level and a sloping section), the exposed edge should be clearly identified by visual contrast and, where necessary, protected by guarding.

See also *Internal ramps, steps, stairs and handrails*, page 83.

## Surface finishes and lighting

• Wall, floor and ceiling surfaces should contrast visually. Doors and / or door frames should contrast visually with adjacent wall surfaces to aid identification.

• Wall and floor surfaces should be chosen to minimise light reflection and sound reverberation, which can be confusing for people with sensory impairments.

• Bold patterns in flooring materials should be avoided. Stripes in particular can be visually confusing and may be mistaken for steps.

• Artificial lighting should provide an even level of illumination of 100 lux and be located where it does not create glare, reflections or silhouettes.

• Glazing positioned at the end of a corridor can cause glare and should be avoided wherever possible.

# 17 Surfaces

The selection of floor, wall and ceiling surfaces is of considerable importance to all building users. Surface characteristics can greatly affect the visual, acoustic and physical environment and need to be individually and collectively considered in order to promote ease of movement, visibility, orientation and acoustic clarity as well as safety.

Hard, reflective surfaces can cause sound reverberation and increased background noise levels, which can make it difficult for some people to hear speech. A mixture of hard and soft surfaces within a room is preferable and helps to provide a balanced acoustic environment.

## Floors

- Floor surfaces should be firm, level and slip-resistant. Floor finishes should be suitable for foot and wheeled traffic.

- Where there is a change in floor surface, adjacent materials should be level and have a similar level of slip resistance. Where a similar level of slip resistance cannot be provided, the change in surface should contrast visually.

- Entrance matting should be effective at removing dirt and moisture from footwear and wheels. (See also *Entrances*, page 48.)

- The junction between all floor finishes should be flush. All edges should be firmly fixed to avoid potential trip hazards.

- Carpets should have a shallow dense pile. Coir matting, deep pile and excessively grooved carpets should be avoided as they can be difficult for wheelchair users to travel across as well as for pushchairs and trolleys.

- Shiny and reflective floor surfaces should be avoided as they can be visually confusing and create glare. Shiny surfaces may appear to be wet even if they are not and, for this reason, some people will not want to cross them.

- Floor surfaces with bold patterns and highly contrasting colours should be avoided. In particular, bold stripes should not be used as these may be perceived as steps.

- A change in the texture of floor surfaces can usefully warn of potential hazards or impart directional information.

## Walls

- Wall surfaces should be plain, not busy or distracting. This is particularly important in areas such as behind reception counters and enquiry desks where communications are important.

- Shiny and reflective wall surfaces should be avoided as they can be visually confusing and create glare.

- The light reflectance value (LRV) of a wall should be at least 30 points different to the LRV of the floor and ceiling (see box on page 82). The LRV of skirting boards should be similar to that of the wall so that they are perceived correctly as being part of the vertical wall surface (as opposed to part of the floor surface).

- Similarly, LRVs for doors, door frames and architraves, door handles and fixtures such as light switches and other controls should be compared to optimise visual contrast. It is preferred if door frame and architraves visually contrast with the adjacent wall so that the position of the door opening is highlighted when the door is open.

- Textured walls (of fine rather than rough grain) can be used to alert people to the presence of facilities such as WCs or lifts where a key to the understanding of this system has been given in advance.

## Glazed screens and walls

- Full-height glazing forming walls or screens should have manifestation markings at two heights (850mm to 1000mm and 1400mm to 1600mm above floor level) to highlight the presence of the glass.

- Manifestation markings should contrast visually with the background in different lighting conditions and comprise a symbol, broken line or repeated pattern covering at least ten per cent of the glass within each zone. (See also *Glazed doors*, page 57, and *Figure 10.4*, page 57.)

- Glass used for screens at reception desks or payment counters should have a low light reflectance so that visibility through the screen is as clear and unobscured as possible.

- Free-standing edges to glazed screens should have a high-contrast strip to ensure people are aware of the presence of the glass.

## Ceilings

- Avoid the use of reflective and high-gloss ceiling surfaces as these can be visually confusing and give a false impression of the size of the room or space.

## Light reflectance value

The light reflectance value (LRV) of a surface is a measurement of the amount of light that a surface reflects. LRVs are measured on a scale from zero (representing a completely absorbing surface such as a pure black) to 100 (representing a completely reflecting surface such as a pure white).

When selecting the colour and finish of products such as carpets, sheet flooring, paints and coatings, veneers and metal coverings, LRVs should be compared to ensure adequate visual contrast is achieved between surfaces and objects. *Figure 17.1* illustrates the degree of difference between LRVs of adjacent surfaces that will achieve good, acceptable and poor visual contrast.

Optimum visual contrast is achieved with a difference in LRV of 30 points or more. In some circumstances, such as with increased lighting levels (200 lux or more), a difference in LRV of 20 points may be acceptable. In general terms, there should be a greater degree of difference between the LRVs of a small fixture and its background (such as a sign on a door) than between those of adjacent large surfaces (such as a wall and a floor).

Figure 17.1
**Graph showing the effectiveness of differing LRVs for adjacent surfaces**

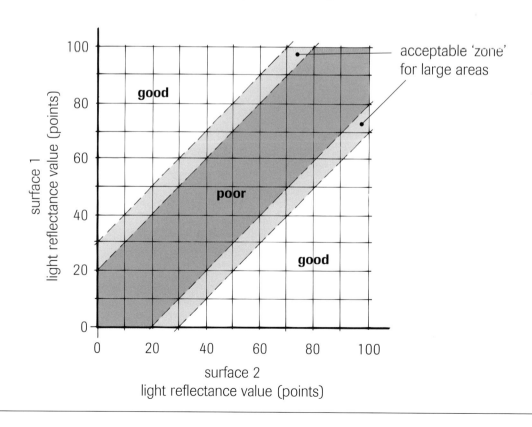

# 18 Internal ramps, steps, stairs and handrails

Ramps, steps, stairs and handrails within buildings should be designed for ease of use and safety for all building users. Design guidance for internal ramps, steps, stairs and handrails is broadly similar to that for external situations.

## Ramps

- In new buildings, internal circulation routes should be level. Where changes of level are unavoidable, such as in existing buildings, ramped access should be available.

- Where the change in level is less than 300mm, a ramp should be provided instead of a single step. Where the change in floor level is 300mm or greater, two or more clearly signposted steps should be provided in addition to a ramp.

- For guidance on ramp widths, gradients, landings, edge protection and lighting. (See also *External ramps*, page 39, and *Figures 6.1* to *6.3*, pages 39–41.)

- Surface finishes of internal ramps should be firm, easy to clean and maintain, and slip-resistant. If ramps are at risk of getting wet, the slip resistance of the surface material should be maintained when wet. Thick carpets should not be used.

## Steps and stairs

- Steps and stairs that are not enclosed should be positioned away from principal circulation routes. Wherever possible, the approach to steps and stairs should require a deliberate change in the direction of travel. (See *Figure 18.1*.)

Figure 18.1
**Stairs positioned away from principal circulation route**

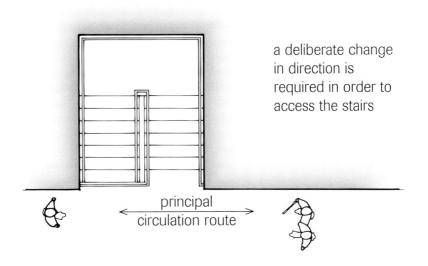

a deliberate change in direction is required in order to access the stairs

principal
circulation route

- For guidance on stair widths, landings, lighting, step nosing identification and profile, refer to *External steps*, page 43, and *Figures 7.1* and *7.2*, page 44 and 45.

- Step risers should be between 150mm and 170mm. Step goings should be between 250mm and 450mm. (Where space is limited in existing buildings, minor deviations from the riser measurements may be acceptable.)

- There should be no more than 12 steps between landings. (In smaller and existing buildings, up to 16 steps between landings may be acceptable.)

- Surface finishes of internal steps and stairs should be firm, easy to clean and maintain, and slip-resistant. If steps and stairs are at risk of getting wet, the slip resistance of the surface material should be maintained when wet. Thick carpets should not be used.

- Surface finishes to steps should visually contrast with landing surfaces to help identify the top and bottom of the flight.

- Where different surface finishes are used for stair landings and steps, the frictional characteristics should be similar to avoid the potential for tripping.

- Tactile hazard warning surfaces are not required at the top and bottom landings of internal steps and stairs. (The frictional characteristics of tactile hazard warning surfaces are markedly different to commonly-used internal floor finishes and, as such, present a significant trip hazard.)

- Spiral stairs and tapered treads are not recommended for stairs used by the general public.

- Open risers should not be used.

- Single steps should be avoided.

## Handrails

- For guidance on handrail design and positioning, refer to *Handrails*, page 46, and *Figure 8.1*, page 46.

# 19 Passenger lifts

The provision of a passenger lift serving all floor levels (including basement floors) is essential in ensuring convenient and comprehensive access to all areas, facilities and services within multi-storey buildings.

## Lift provision

- The number and size(s) of lift should be selected with reference to the size of the building, the likely intensity of use of the lift(s) and the needs of all building users, including staff, customers and visitors.

- BS 5655-6 provides detailed guidance on the selection and installation of new lifts. Passenger lifts should conform to BS EN 81-1, BS EN 81-2 and BS EN 81-70.

- The smallest size of passenger lift suitable for non-domestic buildings has a lift car 1100mm wide × 1400mm deep and is able to accommodate one wheelchair user and one other person (*Figure 19.1*). Wheelchair users are not able to turn around in this size of lift and therefore need to reverse into or out of the lift car if there is a door on only one side.

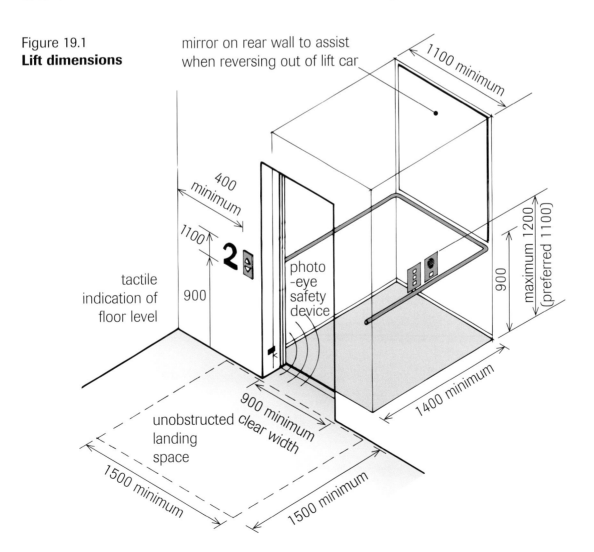

Figure 19.1
**Lift dimensions**

- Larger-size lifts are preferred, where possible, and may in fact be required depending on the building type and use. For example, a lift compartment 2000mm wide by 1400mm deep will accommodate most types of wheelchair together with several other standing passengers. Wheelchair users should be able to turn around within a lift car of this size.

- For guidance on the size of lifts for sports buildings, refer to Sport England's *Accessible Sports Facilities.*

- If it suits the building layout, the provision of doors on opposite sides of the lift can be useful and avoids the need for wheelchair users to reverse into or out of the lift car.

- The location of the lift(s) should be clearly identified from the building entrance. Routes to the lift should be direct, free of obstructions and step-free.

## Lift landing areas

- Lift landings should be provided immediately in front of all lift doors and be level, unobstructed and at least 1500mm × 1500mm. It is preferred if lift landings are separate from circulation routes and not located opposite a flight of stairs.

- Lift call buttons should contrast visually with their mounting plate and the mounting plate should contrast with the wall. Symbols on the call buttons should be embossed and the buttons should illuminate when pressed.

- Call buttons should be mounted 900mm to 1100mm above floor level and at least 400mm from any return wall.

- Visual and audible indication of lift arrival and direction of travel should be clear from any position within the lift landing. Where there is more than one lift, sufficient time should be allowed to enable people to reach the relevant lift.

- The floor area outside the lift and lift car doors should visually contrast with the adjacent walls.

- Visual and tactile indication of floor level should be provided adjacent to the lift call buttons and also opposite the lift doors.

## Lift door and interior

- Power-operated horizontal sliding doors should provide an effective clear width of at least 900mm for lifts 1100m wide × 1400mm deep or 1100mm for lifts 2000mm wide × 1400mm deep.

- Lift doors should remain open long enough for people who are slow moving to enter and leave the lift car comfortably.

- Lift doors should incorporate a light-curtain or photo-eye safety device between 25mm and 1800mm above the door sill to prevent the door from closing if a person or object remains within the door opening.

- Control panels should be located on the side wall of the lift car within the reach of people seated and standing. In lift cars 2000mm wide × 1400mm deep and larger, duplicate controls should be provided on both side walls.

- Lift car controls should meet the requirements of BS EN 81-70 and be arranged either horizontally or vertically, within the preferred height range of 900mm to 1100mm (maximum 1200mm). The provision of extra large controls should be considered for increased accessibility (as set out in Annex G of BS EN 81-70).

- Lift buttons should incorporate embossed symbols and numbers which contrast visually with the face plate and surroundings and provide visual and audible feedback when pressed.

- Audible announcements and visual displays should be available within the lift car to indicate the floor level reached.

- A handrail should be provided to at least one side of the lift car, positioned 875–925mm above floor level, with a cross-section between 30mm and 45mm (radius minimum 10mm) and minimum 35mm clearance to the wall. Handrail-ends should return to the wall.

- An emergency communication system should be provided in all lifts and meet the requirements of BS EN 81-28. It should be easy to use and comprise an intercom with push-button activation (not a telephone handset) and volume control as well as an inductive coupler. It is useful to have a second emergency communication system near the floor for use by a person who has fallen.

- Alarm buttons in lifts should be fitted with a visual acknowledgement that the alarm bell has sounded.

- The floor of the lift car should have a similar level of slip resistance to the lift landings to avoid the potential for slips and trips.

- It is preferred if the lift car floor surface is light in colour (or has a high light reflectance value). Dark floor surfaces can be wrongly perceived as being an open lift shaft and are a source of anxiety for some people.

- Lighting and surfaces within the lift car should minimise glare, reflection, confusing shadows and pools of light and dark. Lights adjacent to control panels are not recommended because they can make it difficult for people to read the controls.

- Lifts with a door on only one side and a lift car 1100mm wide × 1400mm deep should have a mirror on the wall opposite the door to enable people to see behind them as they reverse out onto the landing. The bottom edge of the mirror should be no lower than 900mm. (Full-height mirrors should not be used as they can make the lift car appear to be a through corridor.)

- The provision of a fold-down seat, 500mm high, should be considered for larger lifts.

- Areas of glass, such as glass lift doors, should be identifiable by visually impaired people and incorporate suitable markings for safety and visibility. Refer to *Glazed doors*, page 57. Glass floors to lifts should not be used.

- Lifts that are designated for emergency evacuation should be fitted with an independent power supply, be located within a fire-protected shaft and have controls and other features set out in BS 9999. (See also *Means of escape*, page 129.)

# 20 Platform lifts

Platform lifts offer an alternative means of vertical travel in existing buildings where it is not possible to install a passenger lift. Platform lifts comprise a guarded vertical lifting platform suitable in size for conveying one wheelchair user and one other person. They are typically much slower to operate than passenger lifts and rely on continuous pressure controls; therefore they cannot be considered as providing a comparable level of service to passenger lifts. Platform lifts can be installed externally as well as internally and may be non-enclosed, partially enclosed or enclosed.

## General provisions

- Platform lifts should be located adjacent to the stair with which they are associated. Access to the platform lift should be direct and unobstructed.

- External platform lifts should be sufficiently protected from the weather, particularly in relation to electrical components.

- For guidance on minimum lift platform and door sizes, refer to *Table 20.1*. A larger platform may be required to accommodate electrically-powered wheelchairs and scooters (subject to a maximum area of two metres squared). The provision of a fold-down seat will benefit a broader range of potential users.

- Gates and doors to platform lifts must open outwards and be self-closing. Gates and doors may be power-assisted (refer to *Power-operated doors*, page 65).

- The locking mechanism for gates and doors must be linked to the platform lift mechanism to prevent them from being opened when the platform is not aligned with the corresponding landing floor.

**Table 20.1**
**Platform sizes and door arrangements**

| Minimum platform size | Capacity | Position of doors (or gates) | Minimum clear width of doors (or gates) |
|---|---|---|---|
| 1100mm wide × 1400mm deep | One wheelchair user with a companion | Doors on opposite or adjacent sides is acceptable | 900mm |
| 900mm wide × 1400mm deep | One unaccompanied wheelchair user | Doors on opposite sides (this platform size is not suitable for doors on adjacent sides) | 800mm |

- Controls may comprise push buttons, joysticks or rocker switches and should be easy to use and identifiable both visually and by touch. Text and symbols should be embossed and the active part of controls should contrast visually with the faceplate or mounting surface.

- Controls should be positioned on the side wall of the lifting platform, at a height between 900mm and 1100mm, and no closer than 400mm to the end walls, doors or gates.

- Audible as well as visual indication should be provided within the platform lift and at each landing level to denote the floor level reached and lift arrival.

- A two-way emergency voice communication system should be provided and should be easy to identify and use.

- A handrail should be provided to at least one wall (or guarding), positioned 875–925mm above floor level, with a cross-section between 30mm and 45mm (radius minimum 10mm) and minimum 35mm clearance to the wall (increased to 100mm if the handrail is adjacent to a moving surface). Handrail-ends should return to the wall.

- Wherever possible, the floor of the lifting platform should be level with the floor at the lowest boarding point. If this is not practical (such as in some retrofit situations), a shallow access ramp should be provided to bridge any difference in level greater than 15mm.

## Non-enclosed platform lifts

- Non-enclosed and partially enclosed platform lifts should conform to BS 6440:2011.

- Gates guarding the upper floor area served by a non-enclosed platform lift should be at least 1100mm high. If higher than 1100mm, the gates (or door) should incorporate a vision panel.

- Fixed guarding and gates to platforms travelling vertically up to 1000mm should be 900mm to 1100mm high and include a mid-rail and 100mm high kickplate.

- Fixed guarding and gates to platforms travelling vertically more than 1000mm should be at least 1100mm high and be designed to include a 100mm high kickplate plus vertical bars or solid panels such that a 100mm diameter sphere cannot pass through.

Figure 20.1
**Non-enclosed / short-rise platform lifts**

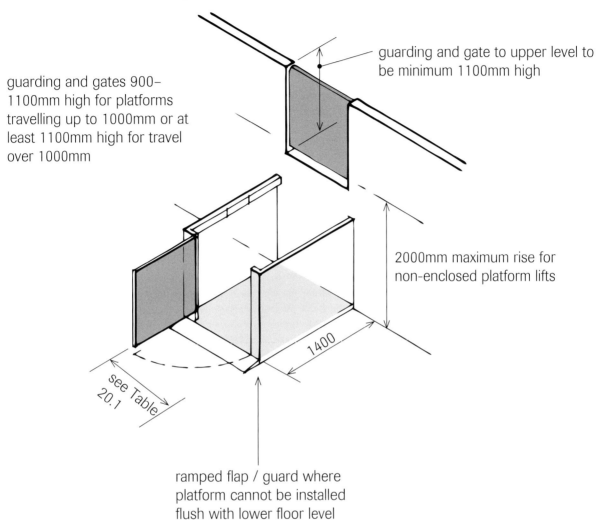

guarding and gate to upper level to be minimum 1100mm high

guarding and gates 900–1100mm high for platforms travelling up to 1000mm or at least 1100mm high for travel over 1000mm

2000mm maximum rise for non-enclosed platform lifts

1400

see Table 20.1

ramped flap / guard where platform cannot be installed flush with lower floor level

## Enclosed platform lifts

• Enclosed platform lifts should conform to BS EN 81-41:2010.

• Platform lifts are recommended to be enclosed where the vertical travel distance exceeds 2m and / or the lift penetrates a floor (*Figure 20.2*).

## Inclined platform stairlifts

• Inclined platform stairlifts may – in exceptional circumstances – be suitable in existing buildings where it is not feasible to install either a passenger lift or vertical-rise platform lift. They are not appropriate in new buildings. Although designed to be operated independently, they are only suitable where users can be instructed in their safe use and under management supervision. Like vertical-rise platform lifts, disadvantages include slow travel speed and the need for the application of continuous pressure on controls, which may be difficult for some people.

• Minimum clear dimensions for the platform of an inclined platform stairlift are 800mm wide by 1250mm deep. A clear access route 800mm wide should be provided at the top and bottom landing.

• The stairlift should have controls that are designed to prevent unauthorised use and an alarm. A means of communication with building staff is recommended should assistance be required in using the equipment.

• In a building with a single stairway, the required clear stair width for means of escape should be maintained between the stairlift rail and opposite handrail and a minimum clear width of 600mm maintained when the platform is folded down (or in use). Early consultation with the fire officer is recommended if an inclined stairlift is proposed.

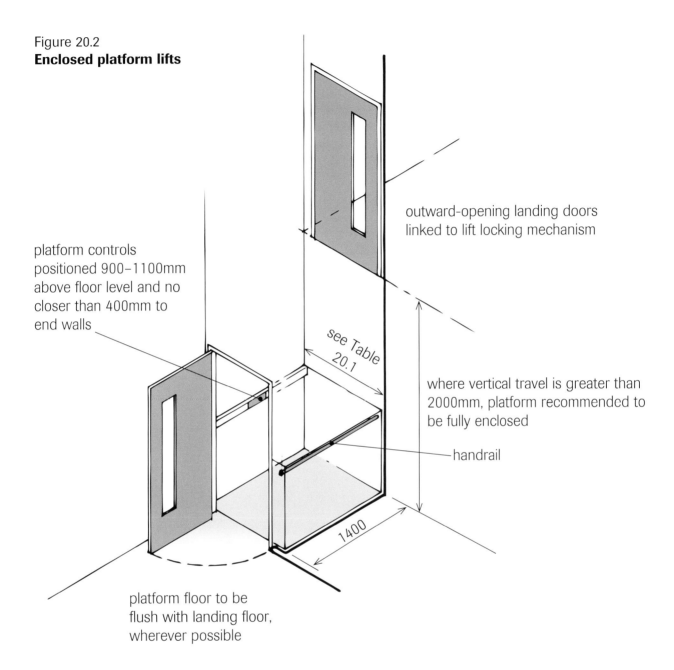

Figure 20.2
**Enclosed platform lifts**

outward-opening landing doors
linked to lift locking mechanism

platform controls
positioned 900–1100mm
above floor level and no
closer than 400mm to
end walls

see Table 20.1

where vertical travel is greater than
2000mm, platform recommended to
be fully enclosed

handrail

1400

platform floor to be
flush with landing floor,
wherever possible

# 21 Sanitary facilities

Suitable and conveniently located sanitary facilities that are easy to identify should be provided for everyone likely to use a building. This will involve the provision of a range of facilities, some of which may be unisex and some of which may be single-sex. Appropriate provision will vary according to type and size of building and use patterns.

## Overall provision

• At least one unisex accessible WC should be provided in each location where sanitary accommodation is provided for use by customers, visitors or employees. A unisex accessible WC should be located close to the entrance and / or waiting area of a building.

• The number and location of unisex accessible WCs depends on the size and use of the building. An employee who is a wheelchair user should not have to travel more than 40m on one level or more than 40m total horizontal distance (when using a passenger lift to travel between floors) to an accessible WC.

• Where there is space for only one WC in smaller buildings, it should be an enlarged unisex accessible WC and comprise all the sanitaryware and accessories provided in a corner-arrangement accessible WC plus a standing-height washbasin, as shown in *Figure 21.1*.

• In single-sex toilet areas, at least one cubicle in a group of cubicles should be suitable for ambulant disabled people, as shown in *Figure 21.2*.

• In large public buildings, Changing Places toilets (see page 102) with adult hoist and changing bench facilities should be provided in addition to standard accessible WCs.

Figure 21.1
**Enlarged unisex accessible WC**

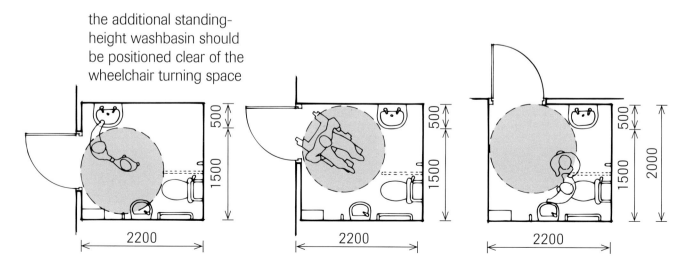

the additional standing-height washbasin should be positioned clear of the wheelchair turning space

Figure 21.2
**WC compartment for ambulant disabled people**

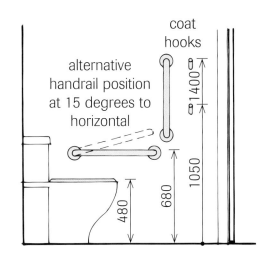

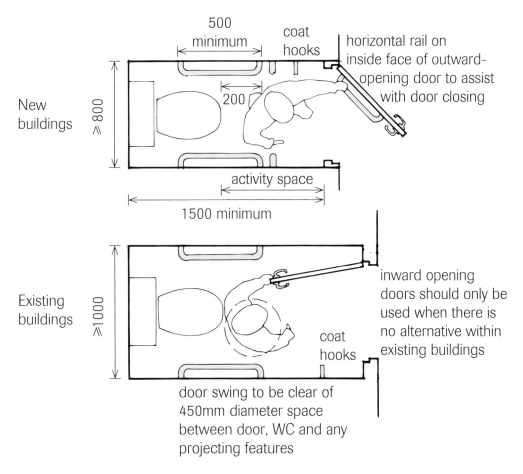

New buildings

Existing buildings

- Accessible WCs may also be provided in single-sex toilet areas, but this should always be in addition to a unisex accessible WC.

- In male toilet areas, at least one urinal in a series of urinals should be accessible to wheelchair users and people of shorter stature, as shown in *Figure 21.3*.

Figure 21.3
**Accessible urinals**

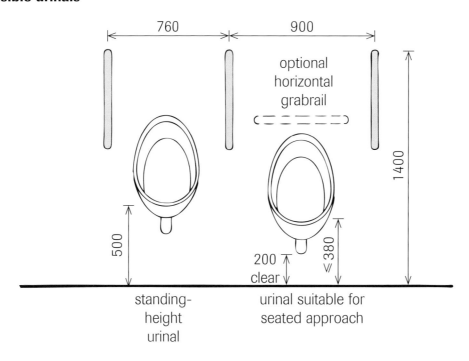

standing-height urinal

urinal suitable for seated approach

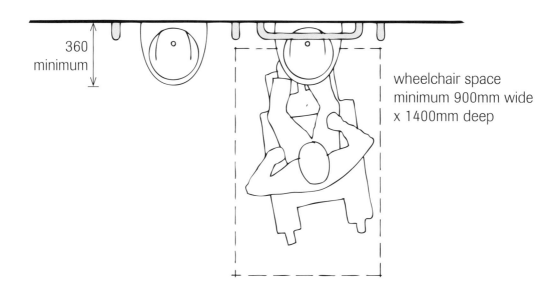

wheelchair space minimum 900mm wide x 1400mm deep

- The provision of a lower-height washbasin in a suite of washbasins in single-sex washrooms is recommended.

## Doors and locks

- Doors to WC cubicles and wheelchair-accessible unisex compartments should, preferably, open out. If they open in, they should not encroach unduly on usable space. Reduced-swing doors could be used where space outside is restricted.

- Outward-opening doors should have a horizontal rail on the inside face to help people close the door.

- Cubicle doors and doors to accessible WCs and Changing Places toilets should not be fitted with mechanical self-closing devices.

- Doors to sanitary accommodation should be capable of being opened in an emergency, such as by using an emergency release bolt and pivot hinge and / or a privacy bolt that can be opened from the outside.

- Easy-to-use privacy locks, clearly indicating if a facility is in use, should be provided and highlighted with a change in colour (red / white or red / green) as well as the text Vacant and Occupied.

- Accessible toilets should be clearly signed using the *International Symbol for Access* (see page 111).

## Sanitaryware and accessories

- Flooring throughout sanitary accommodation should be slip-resistant, especially when wet. Shiny wall and floor surfaces should be avoided as they can create confusing reflections and glare.

- Fixtures and fittings within sanitary accommodation should contrast visually with background surfaces to aid identification.

- The recommended height from the floor to the top of the WC seat is 480mm for WCs used by adults.

- Wall-mounted handrails should be 32mm to 35mm in diameter and have a 50mm to 60mm clearance between the wall surface and handrail. They should be easy to grip, even when wet.

- Drop-down support rails should be capable of being firmly held when folded up against the walls, but easy to release when required. (Rails without support struts are preferred.)

- All fixed handrails and drop-down support rails should be firmly fixed to a robust wall capable of supporting at least 171kg.

- Clothes hooks are recommended at two heights – 1050mm and 1400mm. They should be positioned where they will not present a potential obstruction.

- Toilet paper and paper towel dispensers should be designed for single-hand operation.

- Consider privacy screens for urinals where grabrails are not provided.

- A low-level urinal and washbasin for children and people of short stature in male WCs are recommended.

## Heating, lighting and water supply

- Washbasin taps should be easy to use (sensor-operated or single lever-action) with a thermostatic mixer that delivers water at a temperature not exceeding 43 degrees C.

- Water supply and waste pipes should be concealed or neatly boxed-in so that they cannot be touched. Pipe boxing should not encroach into transfer space or obstruct access to the washbasin or WC.

- Radiators (and other heat emitters) should be either screened or have their exposed surfaces maintained at less than 43 degrees C. They should not encroach into the minimum room dimensions or into any transfer space for wheelchair users.

- Lights that are individually controlled should either have a large wall-switch or a visually contrasting pull cord terminating 900mm to 1000mm above floor level and be positioned 150mm from the edge of the door and wall surface.

- Emergency lighting should be provided to sanitary accommodation to prevent people being left in the dark in the event of a power failure.

## Alarms

- Emergency assistance alarm systems linked to a staffed area of the building should be provided and incorporate visual and audible indicators to confirm that an emergency call has been received, a reset control reachable from the WC or from a wheelchair, and a signal that is different from the fire alarm.

- Alarm pull cords should be coloured red and have two bangles 50mm in diameter, one positioned 800mm to 1000mm above floor level and the other on the end of the cord with a clearance of 100mm to the floor.

- These should be checked daily to ensure they have not been tied up.

- Any fire alarms should emit a visual and audible warning to occupants of WCs. (See also *Emergency alarms*, page 132.)

- Alarms should be regularly maintained and tested for good working order.

- Staff should be trained to respond to the alarm, with staff response time regularly checked. As WC emergency alarms are unlikely to be in regular use, care should be taken to ensure that staff can recognise the alarm and are aware of procedures.

## Unisex accessible corner WC

- The room size and layout should accord with *Figure 21.4a*. Wherever possible, the room size should be larger than the minimum dimensions 1.5m × 2.2m. If it is the only WC available it should be a minimum of 2m x 2.2m.

- Where more than one unisex accessible WC is provided in a building, the layout should be handed to offer a choice of right-hand or left-hand transfer. Where the arrangement is for left-hand transfer, this should be indicated on signage.

- The positioning of all sanitaryware and associated fixtures relative to the manoeuvring space in accessible WCs is critical for independent use. Dimensional guidance should be strictly adhered to.

- The toilet flush handle should be easy to operate and mounted on the transfer side of the cistern within easy reach. A lever-type flush is recommended.

- For specific guidance on the provision of accessible WCs in sports buildings, refer to Sport England's *Accessible Sports Facilities*.

Figure 21.4a
**Unisex accessible WC – corner layout**

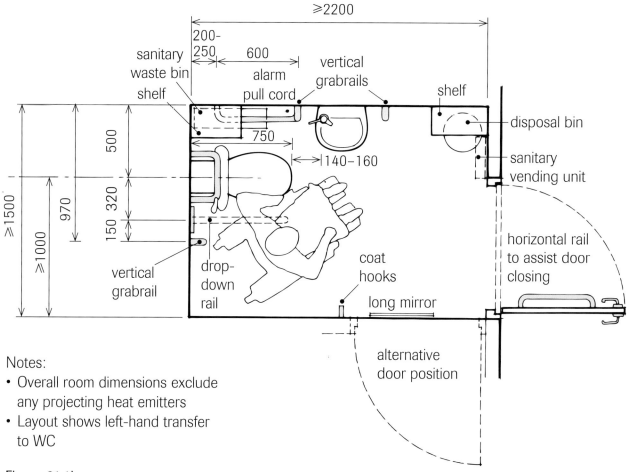

Notes:
- Overall room dimensions exclude any projecting heat emitters
- Layout shows left-hand transfer to WC

Figure 21.4b
**Unisex accessible WC – corner layout**

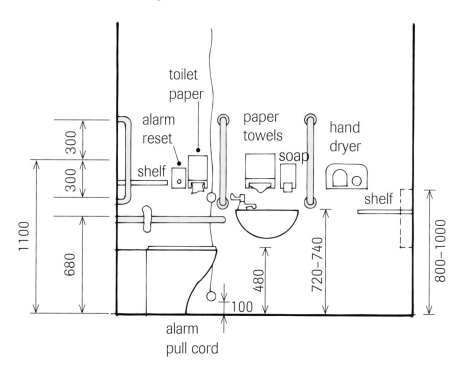

## Accessible baby changing facilities

Baby changing facilities, where provided, should be accessible and located separately from single-sex sanitary accommodation so that they are available jointly to male and female parents and carers. Fold-down baby changing tables should not be located in unisex accessible WCs.

- Baby changing rooms should be minimum 2000mm × 2000mm.

- A baby changing bench should be at a fixed height of 750mm or be height-adjustable. A chair should be available for use with a fixed-height bench.

- The washbasin should have a rim height of 720mm to 740mm above floor level. Soap dispensers and hand drying facilities should be positioned close to the washbasin with the underside 800mm to 1000mm above floor level.

- A nappy vending machine should be provided with the controls and dispensing drawer no higher than 1000mm above floor level.

- A waste bin for nappy disposal should be available and preferably recessed into the wall so as not to obstruct manoeuvring space.

Figure 21.5
**Accessible baby changing room**

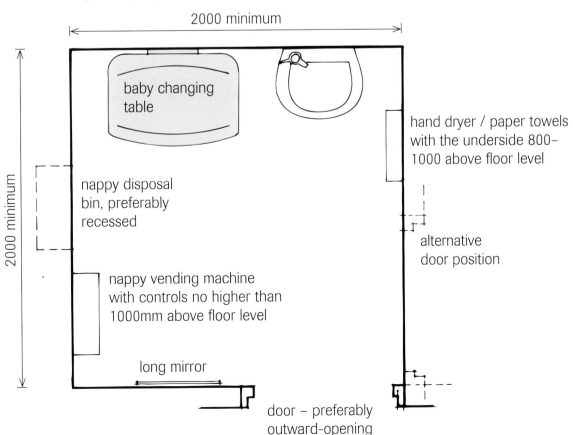

## Prayer washing facilities

Prayer washing facilities provided in mosques, and in association with prayer rooms in other buildings such as workplaces, education establishments and airports, should be accessible to disabled people. Wudu, the ritual washing performed by Muslims in preparation for formal prayers, involves washing of the face, hands and feet in running water.

- Male and female prayer washing facilities should be segregated and each should be accessible to disabled people.

- At least one washing position in each prayer washing facility should have a step-free floor surface and sufficient space to enable a wheelchair user to approach, wash and turn in a wheelchair.

- Wall-mounted grabrails and drop-down support rails should be provided to each side of the wheelchair-accessible washing position.

- The floor surface in prayer washing facilities is likely to be splashed and should therefore be non-slip and well drained.

- Consider the provision of seats at different heights (or adjustable in height) for the washing positions.

- Coat hooks and hand dryers should be provided at a range of heights.

- Storage for footwear should be provided at a range of heights and with sufficient capacity to cater for the expected number of people.

## Changing Places toilets

Changing Places (CP) toilets provide sanitary accommodation for people with complex and multiple disabilities who require more space and additional facilities in order to use the toilet comfortably and with appropriate assistance. CP toilets include a peninsular toilet, a height-adjustable wash hand basin, a height-adjustable changing bench, a hoist and sufficient space to facilitate easy access and transfer between facilities.

CP toilets are designed and provided for people who cannot use standard accessible toilets. CP toilets should be designated for use by disabled people who need assistance and the specific facilities provided. The full range of single-sex, accessible toilets and baby changing facilities should be provided in addition.

CP facilities should be provided in larger public buildings (including retail, sports, leisure and entertainment venues, transport interchanges and healthcare buildings), education establishments and large hotels.

## Location, access and identification

- The location of a CP toilet should be clearly signed and access to it should be convenient and direct. All routes between the building entrance, CP toilet and other key facilities should be accessible and free of obstructions.

- Wherever practicable, a CP toilet should be located close to a customer service desk or within a staffed suite of public conveniences so that the facility can be actively managed and controlled.

- Changing Places toilets should be clearly identified using the Changing Places symbol (*Figure 21.6*).

Figure 21.6
**Changing Places symbol**

- Signage should be provided adjacent to CP toilets to identify the location of the nearest unisex accessible toilet and baby changing facilities so that the facility is not used by people who are able to access other facilities.

- Where a CP toilet is provided, the Changing Places Consortium should be informed so that information relating to the facility can be displayed on the website.

## Room layout and equipment

- The overall arrangement and position of equipment in a CP toilet is critical in ensuring that people are able to access and use the facilities with ease. *Figures 21.7* and *21.8* illustrate one possible room arrangement.

- It is important to consult local user groups, organisations and relevant health professionals (such as occupational therapists) to identify the most appropriate equipment and fittings for installation. It is essential for users to have access to suitable equipment, including hoists with sling compatibility.

Figure 21.7
**Changing Places toilet (plan view)**

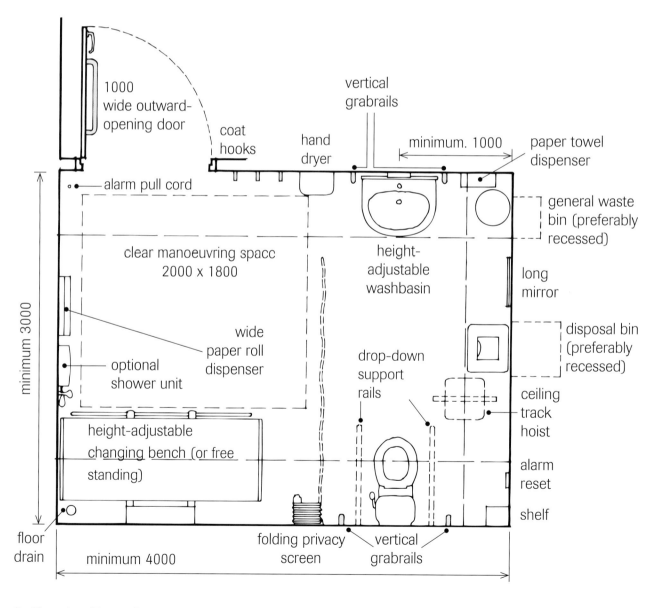

© Changing Places Consortium

Figure 21.8
**Changing Places toilet (wall elevation)**

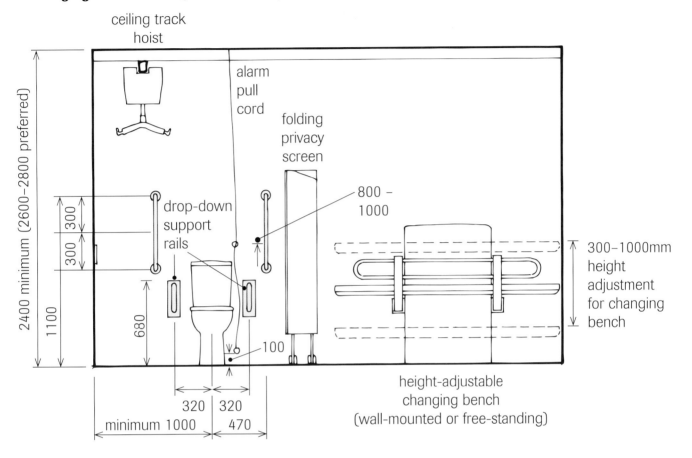

## WC Fixtures

• The toilet should be in a peninsular arrangement with sufficient space for an assistant on both sides and positioned to enable convenient transfer to and from a wheelchair or the ceiling track hoist.

• The toilet should have a backrest and seat (not gap-fronted). All fixings should be robust as considerable pressure will be applied during transfer.

• A shelf for colostomy bags should be positioned where it will not obstruct use of handrails or other equipment, but where it is within reach of a person using the toilet. The shelf should be at least 100–150mm deep and 400mm wide, positioned 950mm above floor level.

• Wall-mounted vertical handrails and drop-down support rails should be provided to both sides of the WC to offer support to people while transferring and while seated.

• Fixed handrails should be tubular in cross-section (32mm to 35mm in diameter), minimum 600mm long, and with a clearance of 50mm to 60mm between the wall and handrail.

- Drop-down support rails should be capable of being firmly held when folded up against the walls, but easy to release when required. Drop-down rails that are height-adjustable are preferred and offer improved safety for users.

- It is essential that handrail and support rail fixings as well as the building structure are strong enough to support the weight of a person.

- A height-adjustable washbasin (adjustable within the range 580mm to 1030mm above floor level) should be provided to enable use in either a seated or standing position. The washbasin should be large and provide a clear knee space below the bowl.

- Washbasin taps should be easy to operate and adjust, such as lever handle mixer taps.

- Hand drying facilities (preferably including both paper towels and a hot air dryer) should be provided close to the washbasin.

- A privacy curtain or screen (either free-standing or retractable) should be available. This provides privacy for people who, having been assisted onto the toilet, are able to use it unaided, and to enable an assistant to use the toilet in privacy when they are not able to leave the person they are accompanying alone outside the room.

### Hoist equipment
- A ceiling track hoist with full-room cover is recommended to enable a person to make full use of all facilities. The hoist should confirm to BS EN ISO 10535 and have a minimum safe working load of 200kg. The ceiling structure should be sufficient to support the hoist.

- Hoists should offer maximum compatibility with a range of sling types and manufacturers. It is essential that local user groups and organisations are consulted to identify the most appropriate hoist as users provide their own slings for use.

- Hoists should incorporate easy-to-use handset controls with auxiliary controls on the motor unit, an emergency lowering and emergency stopping device, soft-start and soft-stop motor control and a return-to-charge feature in a convenient location within the room.

- Hoists should be regularly inspected, serviced and maintained in order to ensure safe, effective use. Hoists are subject to the Lifting Operations and Lifting Equipment Regulations 1998. (See also *Building management*, page 123.)

### Changing benches
- An adult-size height-adjustable changing bench (either fixed or free-standing) should be provided to enable people to lie down while being changed or showered. The changing bench should be at least 1800mm long, 800mm wide and adjustable in height within the range 300mm to 1000mm above floor level.

- The changing bench is recommended to have a minimum safe working load of at least 200kg, although a greater capacity is preferable for a range of users.

- The height-adjustment should be mains-powered (or battery-powered for free-standing benches) and easy to operate.

- The changing bench should have a comfortable surface that is suitable for changing and showering. It is preferable if the bench has an adjustable backrest at one or both ends to improve comfort.

- A dispenser with a wide paper roll (to cover the bench for each user) should be wall-mounted adjacent to the head of the changing bench, within easy reach of an assistant.

- A shower area is recommended in a Changing Places toilet to enable people to be cleansed after using the WC or while being changed. The shower unit should be wall-mounted adjacent to the changing bench where it can be easily reached and operated by an assistant or by a person seated on a shower chair.

- The floor in a Changing Places toilet should be a 'wet room' floor. The shower area should be very slightly sloped (maximum gradient 1:50) to enable water to drain towards a floor outlet, which should be recessed into the floor structure and have a flush cover.

- The shower controls should be easy to operate and be positioned between 750mm and 1000mm above floor level. The shower head should be detachable and mounted on a flexible hose which should be long enough to reach along the changing bench. It should also have a vertical mounting bar for use in conjunction with a shower chair and be adjustable in height between 1050mm and 1850mm above floor level.

- An assistance alarm should be provided, with pull cords and reset button positioned in the locations shown in *Figures 21.7* and *21.8*. The pull cords, coloured red, should each have two bangles 50mm in diameter, one positioned 800mm to 1000mm above floor level and the other on the end of the cord with a clearance of 100mm to the floor. The reset button should be positioned with the underside 800mm to 100mm above floor level and give audible and visual acknowledgement that the alarm has been activated.

- The water temperature for the washbasin and shower should be adjustable, but should not exceed 43 degrees C at the outlet.

For further detailed guidance on the planning and design of CP toilets, refer to *Changing Places: A practical guide* and the Changing Places website: www.changing-places.org.

To register your Changing Places toilet and for further information contact the Changing Places Consortium.

# 22 Wayfinding, information and signs

People orientate themselves and navigate their way around buildings and external spaces by referring to many different types of information within the environment.

A logical building layout gives its own clues as to the location of particular services, such as a reception desk close to an entrance and a lift adjacent to stairs. Views from windows or into atria are useful reminders of location, and changes in construction materials can give tactile, visual and auditory clues to help people differentiate between areas of a building. Well-designed visual signage is important, but so too is the provision of tactile and audible information. For some buildings or external areas maps, models and electronic navigation systems may be appropriate. All of these features are important and all support independent access to and use of buildings and spaces.

## Layout, features and landmarks

• Ensure building layouts and the arrangement of external facilities are as logical as possible. Entrance and exit routes should be obvious.

• Consider the use of landmark features at intervals in larger buildings and in open areas as a navigation aid.

• In multi-storey buildings, position key facilities such as toilets and reception areas in similar locations on each floor level.

• Consider colour coding to signal where certain features are located. For example, the walls within core areas containing stairs, lifts and WCs could be painted a particular colour to aid orientation.

• Use visual contrast to differentiate between floor, wall and ceiling surfaces, door surrounds and decorative features to help define the size and shape of rooms. (See also *Surfaces*, page 80.)

• Where a building relies upon its own vocabulary of textured surfaces to convey information, a key should be provided at a central information point.

## Provision and location of signs

• Signage systems should be considered at an early stage in the design process, be logical and consistent and take into account the different needs of all potential building users.

• Information and directional signs should be provided in locations such as entrance foyers, reception areas, lift landings and junctions in circulation routes and to highlight key facilities such as toilets, waiting areas, refreshment facilities and help-desks.

• Signage should clearly distinguish accessible routes and accessible emergency exits.

• The style, layout, positioning and colour of a signage system should be consistent throughout a building.

• Directional signage should be sufficiently comprehensive to enable a person to locate a particular facility and then to return to their starting point or to another named exit. It should not be assumed that people will be able to retrace their steps.

## Visual signs

• Lettering, symbols and pictograms should contrast visually with the signboard and the signboard should contrast visually with its background or mounting surface. Where the signboard and background are similar in colour, a visually contrasting border could be used.

• The use of light coloured lettering, symbols and pictograms on a dark background is preferred, and the two colours should have a difference in LRV of 70 points. (See *Light reflectance value*, page 82.)

• Words and sentences should be simple, short, consistent and easy to understand.

• Text should be in a sans serif typeface.

• Single words or sentences should start with a capital letter and continue in lower case. Words entirely in upper case should be avoided.

• Directional signs should be firmly fixed and positioned where they will not cause an obstruction. In areas of the building that are likely to be crowded, signs should be positioned at high level. The minimum headroom below all signs suspended from the ceiling or projecting from the wall should be 2300mm.

Figure 22.1
**Sign design detail**

• Embossed symbol and text
• Braille message and locator

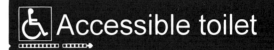

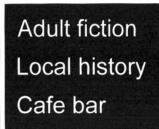

• Locations listed and aligned left where no arrows are used
• Effective visual contrast between text, background and border
• Use of capitals and lower case text

• Arrows and text aligned towards the direction of travel

**109**

- Room name signs should generally be placed on the wall adjacent to the leading edge of the door. Exceptions to this are signs to toilets and push / pull signs.

- Informational signs to be read at close range should be located at a suitable height and can be duplicated to suit people at different levels. The recommended range for a wheelchair user is 1000mm to 1100mm and for somebody standing 1400mm to 1700mm (*Figure 22.2*).

- The text height should suit the likely viewing distances (see *Table 22.1*).

- All signs should be well lit. To minimise glare, avoid the use of reflective glass and ensure that the sign has a matt surface.

**Table 22.1**
**Text heights and viewing distances for signs**

| Viewing range | Example | Text height |
|---|---|---|
| Short range | Room name signs, viewed at close range | 15mm to 25mm |
| Medium range | Directional signs | 50mm to 100mm |
| Long range | Building name signs, viewed from a distance | 150mm |

Note: The text height refers to the lower case letter height.

Figure 22.2
**Height and position of signs**

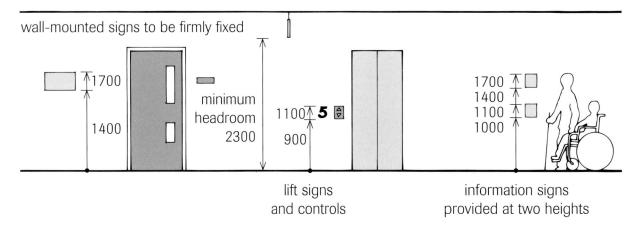

wall-mounted signs to be firmly fixed

1700
1400
minimum headroom 2300
1100 **5** 900
lift signs and controls

1700
1400
1100
1000
information signs provided at two heights

## Symbols and pictograms

- Symbols and pictograms that are easy to recognise should be used to supplement text, wherever possible.

- The size of pictograms and symbols should be as large as possible and at least 100mm high.

- Signs highlighting facilities for disabled people, such as accessible toilets, should incorporate the International Symbol for Access.

- The internationally-recognised public information symbols in *Figure 22.3* should be used to highlight relevant facilities.

## Tactile signs

- Directional signs and signs highlighting key rooms, services and functions in a building should be tactile as well as visual and incorporate embossed letters, pictograms and directional arrows.

- Tactile signs should be positioned where they can be easily reached, preferably between 1400mm and 1700mm above floor level. Tactile signs inclined 45 to 60 degrees from the horizontal are more comfortable to read.

- Embossed text should be in a sans serif typeface. For text 15mm high, characters should be raised 1mm to 1.5mm above the surrounding surface and have a stroke width between 1.5mm and 2mm. Larger text should have a proportionately larger stroke width.

Figure 22.3
**Standard public information symbols**

international symbol for access, denoting facilities which are
fully accessible

facilities for blind and partially sighted people

equipment to enhance microphone sound for people who wear hearing aids fitted
with a 'T' switch

equipment to enhance microphone sound via an infrared receiver

textphone facilities

## Braille

- The use of Braille to supplement embossed text and symbols on tactile signage is recommended.

- Grade 1 Braille should be used for single words or short word groupings on signs, for example Reception or Upper Terrace Bar.

- Grade 2 Braille should be used for longer sentences or instructions on signs, for example a description of a picture in a gallery.

- Braille should be positioned directly under its corresponding text and be aligned to the left of the sign. A locator, 1mm to 1.5mm deep, should be provided along the left-hand edge directly in line with the Braille.

- Where the sign includes a directional arrow, a small embossed arrow should be positioned either just before or just after the Braille.

- Braille on a sign should not be framed or be positioned within a raised border as this can cause confusion and distract from the Braille message.

## Tactile maps and models

- Consider the provision of portable tactile maps of the interior layout of buildings and external environments – particularly those of architectural interest – as these are an effective way of conveying information to people with visual impairments.

- For three-dimensional sites and landscapes, also consider the use of tactile models.

- Tactile maps and models should be clear, uncluttered and differentiate effectively between lines, surfaces and features. They should incorporate a key, a north point and bar scale. Audible and Braille instructions may also be appropriate.

## Audible signs and electronic navigation systems

- Consider the provision of talking signs, such as the RNIB React system, for bus and train stations and for outdoor environments such as town centres. The React system uses radio signals emitted from small personal trigger fobs which activate pre-recorded messages from speakers positioned at regular intervals along a route or to highlight particular landmarks. Messages can be used to aid orientation, provide local or tourist information and transmit real-time bus and train departures.

• Consider the use of remote infrared audible signage (RIAS) for internal and external environments. These systems use personal receivers (which can be linked to headsets) to relay announcements and information via infrared transmitters. As with radio systems, RIAS systems can assist with orientation, wayfinding and real-time service information.

• Innovations utilising Global Positioning Systems (GPS), mapping technology and smartphones will offer increasingly sophisticated and valuable electronic navigation systems to a wide range of people and should be incorporated and / or supported wherever feasible.

# 23 Communication systems and acoustics

Communication systems in buildings enable people to gain information, interact with others and make full use of any services provided. They include equipment for personal communications (such as telephones), public address and information systems as well as systems in performance and other venues that enable people to receive amplified sound, translation or audio description via personal receiving equipment or hearing aids.

The layout and physical properties of buildings all contribute to the acoustic characteristics of individual spaces and structures as a whole. They have a significant impact on the effectiveness and clarity of audible communications. In addition, they provide audible references that are particularly beneficial to visually impaired people when navigating their way around a building and when differentiating between adjacent spaces.

## Telephones for public use

• Where telephones (payphones) are provided in buildings for members of the public to use, at least one should be accessible to wheelchair users. If more than one is provided, they should be at different heights. Consider also the provision of text and email payphones in addition to standard telephones.

• Keypads and other controls to accessible telephones should be positioned 750mm to 1000mm above floor level. If the control panel is angled, the telephone can be more easily used by people standing or using a perch seat.

• Telephones should be positioned to enable approach from the front and from both sides to enable flexibility in use. If it is only possible to approach from the front, a knee recess 700mm high and 500mm deep should be provided.

• Keypads should be well lit and contrast visually with the surrounding surface. Buttons should incorporate large embossed numbers and have a raised dot on the number five.

• A shelf should be provided adjacent to all public telephones to enable people to use their own portable textphones.

• All telephones for public use should include ear piece volume control and an ear piece inductive coupler.

• Telephones located within a booth or room should have a clear floor area 1200mm wide × 1850mm deep.

- Provision of a fold-down seat, 450mm to 520mm high with fold-down arms, or a perch seat, 650mm to 800mm high, is beneficial to many people. Fixed support rails should be provided adjacent to any seating.

- Telephone equipment, shelving or counter surfaces, seats and support rails should all contrast visually with background surfaces.

- The location of accessible telephones should be clearly highlighted with tactile signage incorporating the International Symbol for Access and a telephone symbol. (See also *Symbols and pictograms*, page 111.)

## Public address systems

- In buildings where spoken announcements are made, the information conveyed should be consistent with visual information displays. Spoken announcements should be clear and set at a volume that is suitable for the particular environment and circumstances in which it is heard.

- In large spaces, it is preferable to provide a series of speakers positioned at intervals throughout the building rather than having a single speaker operating at high volume.

- Public address systems should be linked to induction loops to benefit people who wear hearing aids fitted with a 'T' switch.

- See also *Audible signs and electronic navigation systems*, page 112.

## Hearing enhancement systems

- Hearing enhancement systems are essential for improving communications and in enabling people who are deaf and hard of hearing to receive amplified sound signals without interference from background noise. Broader benefits are also available using some types of system such as the provision of audio description for visually impaired people and translation voice-over services for speakers of other languages. Soundfield systems offer improved speech intelligibility and room coverage which benefits everyone in a room. The full range of benefits, as well as the characteristics and limitations of each type of system, should be carefully considered.

- Hearing enhancement systems should be provided in rooms used for meetings, lectures, classes, performances, announcements, the viewing of films and presentations and at reception, enquiry, payment and service counters.

- Specialist advice should be sought at an early stage in the design process (and when retrofitting existing buildings) to identify the most appropriate type of equipment for each location. In some situations, the provision of more than one type of system may be required to meet a range of user needs.

- The availability of all hearing enhancement systems should be clearly signed using the relevant public information symbol (see *Figure 22.3*, page 111). Signs should be located on the approach to and within rooms or areas fitted with such systems.

- All hearing enhancement and public address systems should be regularly tested. Tests should include equipment tests as well as user trials.

- In rooms used for multimedia presentations, input sockets to transmitting equipment should be positioned in accessible locations.

- The output from induction loop and infrared systems in public areas (other than systems driven by sound feeds from public address and loudspeaker systems) should have sufficient monitoring equipment to detect microphone faults at an early stage.

**Induction loops**

Induction loop systems convert sound via a microphone into a varying magnetic field, which is converted back to amplified sound via a person's hearing aid (where the induction pick-up facility is selected, such as a 'T' switch). Induction loops are suitable in locations where information is given verbally such as meeting rooms, box offices, ticket counters, banks, post offices, churches and auditoria.

Permanent induction loops can be installed in rooms such as meeting rooms and auditoria and cover the whole area. Counter loops can be used to serve distinct smaller areas such as payment or enquiry desks. Portable loops can be quickly set up in any room not fitted with a permanent loop and offer flexibility in the use of space within a building and meet individual need.

- Some induction loop systems allow sound to be picked up by hearing aid users in adjacent rooms – this is called overspill and may be a problem in multiscreen cinemas, adjacent classrooms, or where confidentiality is required. Careful planning and the possible use of alternative systems may be required in these circumstances.

- Minimise potential magnetic interference from electrical equipment in or adjacent to rooms fitted with induction loops as this can cause interference.

- Minimise the amount of metal in construction materials for rooms fitted with induction loops as large amounts of metal can reduce the field strength.

### Infrared systems

- Infrared hearing enhancement systems convert sound into infrared light signals. Sound is delivered either directly through a receiving headset or via a person's own hearing aid using a small coupling neck loop. Infrared systems can be used for voice-over services such as audio description and translation as well as for amplifying sound.

- Infrared systems are ideally suited to controlled areas such as cinemas, theatres and lecture rooms, where headsets can be borrowed from a central source. Infrared systems are particularly valuable where confidentiality is important as sound cannot be picked up outside the room in which the infrared signals are generated.

- The minimum number of headsets and neck loop receivers should be equivalent to two to three per cent of the total capacity. This proportion should be monitored and additional equipment provided if demand is higher.

- An effective system should be implemented for the storage, issue, return, cleaning and maintenance of headsets and neck loop receivers.

### Radio systems

- Radio systems transmit sound using radio signals to personal receivers. Radio systems enable transmitter and receiver equipment to be switched between channels, which means that overspill from adjacent rooms can be avoided. The system is entirely portable and can operate over distances of up to 60m.

- Radio systems are commonly used in education buildings where pupils move between many different classrooms and carry the equipment with them. Radio systems are also suitable for organised tours, such as where a tour guide describes a room or exhibit to visitors while moving around a building. The tour guide wears a transmitter and visitors who require hearing enhancement wear a receiver. Separate channels can be used for audio description and translation services.

- Ensure the potential for electromagnetic interference and disturbance from other radio signals is minimised.

- In rooms where loudspeakers are installed, microphones should be compatible with radio system receivers.

- As with infrared systems, an effective system should be implemented for the storage, issue, return, cleaning and maintenance of headsets and receivers.

### Soundfield systems

- Soundfield systems improve speech intelligibility and room coverage by augmenting sound via a series of speakers positioned evenly around a room. Soundfield systems ensure sound levels are consistent throughout a room, thereby eliminating situations in which people at the back of a room find it difficult to hear.

- Soundfield systems are commonly found in classrooms where they benefit everyone in the room, including people with a mild hearing loss who do not wear hearing aids. They also benefit the speaker and other participants who are able to use normal conversational speaking voices (not raised voices) in order to be heard.

- Soundfield systems should be linked to induction loop, infrared or radio hearing enhancement systems, where provided, so that the same microphone can be used for both (or all) systems simultaneously.

## Acoustics

- Areas in buildings where communications are important, such as reception desks, should be positioned away from potential sources of noise (both internal and external).

- The impact of traffic noise should be considered when locating openable windows close to busy roads.

- Adequate sound insulation should be provided to all elements of construction to minimise intrusive noise, both from outside the building and from adjacent internal areas.

- Quiet and noisy areas of buildings should be separated with a buffer zone to reduce potential disturbance.

- Minimise reverberation by selecting a balance of hard and soft surfaces within a room or space. Too many hard surfaces will create reverberation which generates background noise and can make it difficult for people to hear.

- Air conditioning units, extractor fans and some heating units can be noisy when in use. They should be positioned where they will not cause a disturbance and should be regularly maintained in order to reduce noise due to wear.

- Incoming mains electrical cabling should be positioned away from public areas in buildings. Mains cabling generates a considerable magnetic field which can cause a loud hum in hearing aids.

# 24 Switches and controls

Switches and controls for services and equipment in buildings should be accessible and easy to use, where individual operation is required. The location and detailing of switches and controls should take into account ease of operation, height, distance from corners, visibility and unobstructed access.

- Controls, switches and mounting plates should contrast visually with their background surface to aid identification.

- Instructions for equipment should be clearly displayed and positioned adjacent to switches or controls where they can be read at close range. Instructions may be duplicated and positioned at two heights to suit people at different levels. (See *Visual signs*, page 109.) Instructions should be tactile as well as visual.

- Electrical power sockets should always be switched and it should be obvious which position is on and which is off.

- The use of large rocker switches for lights should be considered as these are much easier for many people to use.

- Panels with multiple switches should be large enough to allow sufficient space between each switch. This will help to avoid a person inadvertently selecting the wrong switch or depressing two simultaneously. Switches should be clearly labelled and labels should be tactile as well as visual.

- Electrical mains and circuit isolator switches should be clearly labelled, and on and off positions easy to identify.

- Controls and switches that use red to indicate on and green to indicate off should also incorporate text and / or graphics to confirm the switch status. Red and green colours can be difficult for some people to differentiate.

- The operation of switches, sockets and controls should not require the simultaneous use of both hands.

## Position and height

• Switches, sockets and controls should be positioned logically and consistently in relation to doorways, room corners and height above floor level throughout a building.

• Refer to *Figure 24.1* for the recommended height and position of switches and controls.

Figure 24.1
**Heights of switches and controls**

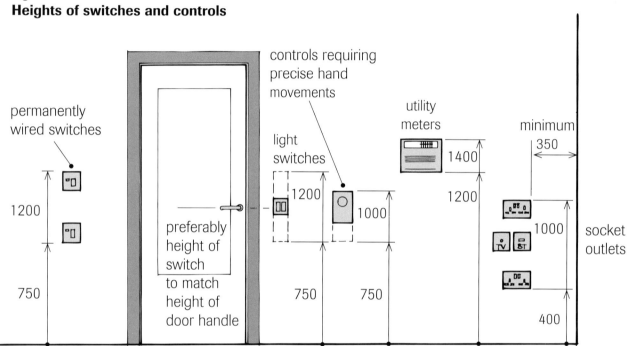

# 25 Lighting

Lighting in and around buildings is essential for visibility and to ensure safe access, circulation and exit for all. Good lighting is critical to effective communications as many people rely on visual information, such as body language, expression, signing and lip-reading, to supplement or replace audible information. As well as contributing to an attractive, welcoming environment, lighting can also be used to accentuate interior colour, tone and texture, which is beneficial for wayfinding.

- All lighting, including natural light, should be controllable and adjustable where possible to suit individual need.

- Artificial lighting levels should take into account the needs of a wide range of building users. In general terms, older people and people who are blind or partially sighted need more light than others.

- Good lighting levels are particularly important in potentially hazardous areas such as stair wells or changes in level along a route.

- In locations such as reception desks, lighting should be positioned to illuminate a person's face in order to assist communications. Lighting should not be positioned behind a receptionist where it will cause them to appear in silhouette as this can make visual communication very difficult.

- In lecture, conference or performance venues, lighting should be positioned to illuminate the speaker's face and to clearly illuminate sign language interpreters.

- Regular cleaning of windows, blinds and lamps ensures sources of natural and artificial light are as effective as possible.

- Passive infrared sensors can be used to detect dim light and activate booster lighting.

- Lights should be positioned where they do not cause glare, reflection, confusing shadows or pools of light and dark. Even levels of illumination along a route or across a room are preferred.

- Positioning lighting in unusual or unexpected places can create shadows and misleading visual effects.

- Uplighters placed above a standing person's eye level can deliver comfortable, glare-free illumination. Uplighters positioned at low level or within the floor should be avoided as they are a potential source of glare.

- Some fluorescent lights create a magnetic field which can cause a humming sound in hearing aids. Lighting of this type should be specified with care and only for locations where it cannot inconvenience people who wear hearing aids.

- Artificial lighting should be compatible with electronic and radio frequency installations.

- Lighting should give good colour rendering for all surfaces within a space. Good colour rendering will optimise light reflectance values (LRVs) and ensure effective visual contrast is achieved where the recommended difference in LRV is selected for adjacent surfaces. (See *Light reflectance value*, page 82.)

- For further guidance on lighting levels and the selection of lamp types, see Society of Light and Lighting, *SLL Code for Lighting*, 2012.

# Building management

- Building management checklist

- Means of escape

# 26 Building management checklist

Accessibility cannot be achieved by good design alone. How a building is managed on a day-to-day basis can have a significant impact, either greatly enhancing usability or rendering a facility inaccessible. Good maintenance practices are also critical in ensuring the building is safe and easy for everyone to use.

The checklist below sets out key practical tasks and checks for external and internal environments. Also highlighted are circumstances in which information should be readily available to building users, sometimes in advance of a visit. Not all items will be relevant to every building and the checklist should not be regarded as exhaustive, but it provides a starting point from which a building-specific checklist can be developed.

## External areas

### Car parking
- Provide information to prospective customers and visitors about the provision and availability of car parking facilities.

- Ensure that non-disabled drivers do not occupy designated parking bays.

- Monitor the use of designated bays and, if necessary due to demand, increase the number of bays.

- Where parking bays are allocated to disabled staff, ensure they are clearly marked as such to discourage use by others.

- Where entry and exit routes in car parks are controlled by barriers, ensure customers are able to contact and communicate with a member of staff who is able to provide assistance.

### Pedestrian routes
- Ensure that external routes, ramps and steps are kept clean, unobstructed and free of surface water, snow and ice and of algae growth.

- Repair loose, uneven and damaged surface materials so they do not present a trip hazard.

- Ensure that parked bicycles do not obstruct access routes and are not chained to the handrails of steps or ramps.

- Regularly trim or cut back vegetation that projects across pedestrian routes within a zone extending from ground level up to 2100mm, and vegetation that obstructs signage, lighting, doorways and important vistas such as at pedestrian crossing points.

- In shared space areas, enforce traffic speed limits, delivery and parking restrictions so that pedestrians can use the space confidently.

- Replace light bulbs and repair damaged lights promptly so that adequate lighting levels are maintained, particularly to externals steps, ramps and access routes.

## Internal areas

### Entrances

- In existing buildings, if a portable ramp is required, ensure it is readily available and removed after use.

- Check that side-hung doors accompanying revolving doors are unlocked and available for use whenever the building is open.

- Regularly test and maintain access control systems to ensure clear and effective communications (visual and audible) between the visitor and staff units.

- Regularly test door opening and closing systems, including push pad devices, presence and motion detectors and any swipe card readers or other security systems. In particular, regularly review the speed and timing of all power-operated devices to ensure they provide sufficient time for people to move towards and through the doorway.

- Ensure that staff are always available to respond to entryphone systems and to provide assistance if required.

### Doors

- Ensure that door ironmongery such as lever handles and hinges are kept clean and free-moving.

- Check and maintain door self-closing devices, ensuring that opening forces are within recommended limits (see also *Doors – opening and closing systems*, page 60).

### Circulation routes

- Keep all internal corridors, lobbies and open-plan circulation routes clear of obstructions, including deliveries.

- Keep spaces in front of lifts, in WCs and in front of signage clear of waste bins, planters and items such as water coolers.

- Maintain adequate space between movable tables and seats in cafés and restaurants to ensure ease of access for all customers.

### Lifts

- Make arrangements for regular statutory tests, inspections and servicing of lifts and platform lifts and ensure these are undertaken when no one will be inconvenienced from the equipment being out of action.

- If lifts or platform lifts are out of action due a breakdown, ensure alternative arrangements are in place and clearly communicated.

- Ensure that the emergency call and communication system in passenger lifts and platform lifts is fully operational and that it is linked to a source of assistance.

- Regularly check that the lift car floor / platform floor aligns with the structural floor at each landing level.

### Surfaces

- Ensure edges of floor coverings are firmly fixed and that edgings and door threshold strips are themselves firmly fixed and do not present a trip hazard.

- Replace worn floor coverings that otherwise may present a trip hazard or fail to provide adequate slip resistance.

- Implement cleaning and polishing regimes that effectively clean floor surfaces but do not leave them shiny or slippery.

- When interiors are redecorated, take care that carefully selected colour schemes and visual contrast are not compromised.

### Sanitary facilities

- If accessible toilets or Changing Places (CP) toilets are required to be kept locked, ensure a key such as a RADAR National Key Scheme key is available to lend close by and that it is obvious to visitors where to obtain the key.

- Ensure staff know where keys for accessible toilets and CP toilets are located and what they are for.

- Regularly check that assistance alarms are fully operational, including the alarm pull cord(s), reset button(s) and responder unit(s).

- Check regularly that alarm cords are fully extended and usable at all times, not tied around grabrails or hooked up out of reach (refer to *Figures 21.4, Unisex accessible WC – corner layout*).

- Building managers should ensure procedures are in place for responding to assistance alarms, that staff are trained in providing appropriate and effective assistance and that there is always someone available to respond to an alarm call.

- In CP toilets, ensure that written instructions for using the equipment are clearly displayed.

- Provide information about the type of hoist connectors and compatible slings where CP toilets are provided.

- Check that all equipment is in full working order.

- Regularly review fastenings to toilet seats, fixed and drop-down rails to make sure they are firm and capable of supporting the weight of a person.

- Restock all toilet areas daily (or more frequently in heavily used facilities) with toilet tissue, soap and hand towels (where provided).

- Ensure that waste bins and sanitary disposal units do not obstruct the transfer space in accessible WCs.

## Building services

### Maintenance and tests

- Arrange for statutory tests, inspections and servicing of lifts, platform lifts, hoists and other equipment.

- Replace light bulbs as soon as they have failed and also fluorescent tubes if they have started to flicker.

### Cleaning

- Regularly clean and maintain mechanical ventilation, air conditioning and heating systems.

- Clean windows regularly to optimise natural daylight to the interior of buildings.

- Ensure window blinds and solar control devices are clean and fully functioning.

## Communications

### Information

- Produce information in a range of formats giving up-to-date details of available facilities and venue accessibility.

- Include in pre-visit information where a RADAR National Key Scheme key is required for accessible toilets and CP toilets and where a key can be obtained.

- Highlight the presence of strobe lighting in advance of a visit or on arrival.

- Provide audio description services in situations where lengthy or complex information is given.

### Hearing enhancement systems

- Ensure that hearing enhancement systems are advertised and that staff are trained in using them.

- Regularly test hearing enhancement systems and public address systems using testing equipment as well as user trials.

- Implement a system for lending headsets for infrared and radio hearing enhancement systems and for retrieval, testing, security and hygiene of headsets.

### Signage

- Ensure that new signs integrate with existing signage, that signs are replaced correctly when removed for redecoration, and that temporary signs are removed when no longer relevant.

- Ensure that maps and models of building interiors are updated when departments move offices or exhibits are relocated.

## Means of escape

### Policy and procedures

- Ensure all emergency exit routes internally and externally are clear and unobstructed at all times and that all final exits are operational and available for use.

- Make sure that access for fire fighting vehicles is available at all times.

- Regularly test the fire alarm system and check that all audible sounders and visible beacons are functional.

- Arrange evacuation tests at regular intervals to ensure that all staff are familiar with emergency evacuation procedures and duties.

- Liaise regularly with disabled members of staff and frequent disabled visitors to agree and review individual personal emergency evacuation plans (*PEEPs*; see also page 131).

# 27 Means of escape

The design of buildings and their surroundings must ensure that everyone is able to escape safely in the event of a fire or emergency. Often, practical measures taken to facilitate easy access into buildings also serve to provide an easy route for escape, such as level door thresholds and ramped as well as stepped access routes, but physical features are not the only consideration. Other critical factors include early warning systems and alarms, consultation and communication, staff training, the provision of assistance and the use of auxiliary aids. All of these aspects must be fully considered at design stage and continually reviewed throughout the life of a building.

In as many situations as possible, the layout and features of a building should enable people to evacuate independently, but where this is not achievable, assistance from staff or the use of auxiliary aids should form part of the overall means of escape. Formulating an effective fire safety management process encompassing all these issues is essential for all buildings.

## Fire safety legislation

In the UK, fire safety legislation requires the person (or people) responsible for managing a building to ensure the safety of everyone who uses it as well as those in the immediate vicinity. The overriding principles of the UK legislation are twofold – reducing the risk of fire and making sure people can escape safely in the event of a fire.

Duties imposed by the legislation include carrying out a fire safety risk assessment as well as implementing and maintaining a fire management plan. This plan must include an emergency evacuation plan addressing the needs of all building occupants, including disabled people. The ultimate aim of the emergency evacuation plan is that everyone is able to leave safely in the event of a fire. Emergency evacuation plans should not rely on the fire and rescue service intervening to successfully evacuate everyone from the building – this is the responsibility of building management.

- In England and Wales, the relevant legislation is the Regulatory Reform (Fire Safety) Order 2005.

- In Scotland, the relevant legislation is Part 3 of the Fire (Scotland) Act 2005 and the Fire Safety (Scotland) Regulations 2006.

- In Northern Ireland, the relevant legislation is Part 3 of the Fire and Rescue Services (Northern Ireland) Order 2006 and the Fire Safety Regulations (Northern Ireland) 2010.

The legislation covering all four UK countries applies to all non-domestic buildings and the common parts of houses in multiple occupation.

Detailed guidance on undertaking fire safety risk assessments and developing fire safety management plans for a wide range of building types is available via www.communities.gov.uk.

## BS 9999:2008 *Code of practice for fire safety in the design, management and use of buildings*

BS 9999 provides comprehensive guidance and recommendations on the design, management and use of buildings in the context of fire safety. Fundamental to the guidance is the understanding that buildings and features in them will be managed, maintained and tested throughout their lifetime and that staff will be adequately trained to put into practice the procedures necessary to bring about the safe evacuation of all occupants.

The guidance in BS 9999 covers all practical planning issues such as the design of escape routes and fire doors, signage, access arrangements for the fire and rescue service, compartmentation, fire detection and alarm systems, emergency lighting, lifts and evacuation lifts. In addition, it provides comprehensive guidance on assessing risk, establishing the risk profile of a building, fire protection systems, the management of fire safety, evacuation strategies, fire training and communications and liaison with the fire and rescue service.

## Building emergency evacuation plans

Fire management plans and emergency evacuation plans must be developed with specific reference to individual circumstances such as building type, building occupants, management organisation, staffing and other factors. There is no one-size-fits-all and it is likely that two different organisations occupying similar buildings will have different management and evacuation plans, as will two similar organisations occupying different buildings. The common thread to all situations is the importance of effective consultation, communication and training.

- Speak to the disabled person and discuss any particular requirements.

- All building users (staff and visitors) should be given the opportunity to identify individual requirements for assistance and / or auxiliary aids in order to exit a building safely.

- Disabled people should be made aware of the options available to them, for example the location of accessible exit routes, the location of refuges and methods for being alerted to an emergency situation.

- Procedures should be established for consulting with disabled staff and regular or known visitors to a building in order to agree an individual escape plan (see PEEPs opposite page).

- Staff responsible for communicating the evacuation plan to disabled visitors should be given disability escape etiquette training.

• Information relating to emergency evacuation should be made available, where necessary, in alternative formats including Braille, large print, audio and in other languages.

• Regular evacuation tests should be carried out, including the provision of assistance and use of auxiliary aids, to ensure that staff are aware of their responsibilities and that actions are well rehearsed.

• After every evacuation test, the outcome should be reviewed and, if necessary, modifications made to improve communications and the effectiveness of the procedures.

## Personal emergency evacuation plans

Personal emergency evacuation plans (PEEPs) are tailored action plans which record how individuals who need assistance during an emergency situation will safely exit a building. PEEPs are an essential component of the overall emergency evacuation plan in any building and may be one of the following types:

**Individual PEEPs** These are person-specific and should be in place for individual disabled members of staff and regular disabled visitors to a building such as students at a college or a member of a congregation in a place of worship. The PEEP should be developed in conjunction with the individual and address individual circumstances. This may include the need for assistance during an emergency evacuation such as wayfinding or the use of auxiliary aids such as vibrating pager alarms.

**Visitor PEEPs** These are also person-specific, but are discussed and agreed between the visitor and staff at the time the disabled visitor makes themselves known to building management, such as a disabled guest in a hotel. Staff should sensitively discuss the emergency evacuation procedures with the visitor to determine if assistance is likely to be required during an emergency situation and how this will be provided. Staff responsible for discussing and agreeing PEEPs with visitors should be appropriately trained, be fully aware of the availability of assistance (in terms of staffing capacity, staff capability and the use of equipment) and be able to implement the necessary actions in the event of an emergency.

**Standard PEEPs** These are generic PEEPs which are applicable to buildings such as shopping malls where the general public do not ordinarily make themselves known to building management. Standard PEEPs should anticipate the needs of as wide a range of people as possible and all staff should be familiar with them. Information relating to emergency evacuation procedures, the location of evacuation lifts, refuges and the provision of assistance should be available to members of the public and clearly displayed in statutory Fire action notices. Building management should ensure that sufficient members of staff are available to implement the evacuation plan, including staff trained in carry-down procedures.

## Emergency alarms

• Early warning of an emergency situation gives all building occupants the best chance of making a safe escape.

• Emergency alarms should be provided throughout a building to alert all occupants in the event of a fire. Alarms should incorporate both audible sounders and visual (flashing) beacons.

• Consider the provision of a vibrating pager system as an alternative (or supplementary) means of alerting people that the alarm has been activated.

• Where visual (flashing) beacons are installed in buildings, a sign stating that this is the case should be displayed clearly at the entrance to warn people who are susceptible to seizures induced by strobe lighting.

# Appendices

## Organisations

**British Standards Institution (BSI)**
Telephone: 020 8996 9001
Email: cservices@bsigroup.com
Website: www.bsigroup.com

**Centre for Accessible Environments**
Tel / textphone: 020 7822 8232
Email: info@cae.org.uk
Website: www.cae.org.uk

**Changing Places Consortium**
For enquiries in England, Wales and
Northern Ireland:
Telephone: 020 7696 6019
Email: changingplaces@mencap.org.uk

For enquiries in Scotland:
Telephone: 01382 385 154
Email: pamischangingplaces@dundee.ac.uk
Website: www.changing-places.org

**Equality and Human Rights Commission
(EHRC)**
Helplines:

*England*
Telephone: 0845 604 6610
Textphone: 0845 604 6620
Fax: 0845 604 6630
Email: englandhelpline@
equalityhumanrights.com

*Scotland*
Telephone: 0845 604 5510
Textphone: 0845 604 5520
Email: scotlandhelpline@
equalityhumanrights.com

*Wales*
Telephone: 0845 604 8810
Textphone: 0845 604 8820
Email: waleshelpline@equalityhumanrights.
com
Website: www.equalityhumanrights.com

**Equality Commission for Northern
Ireland**
Telephone: 028 90 500 600
Textphone: 028 90 500 589
Enquiry line: 028 90 890 890
Email: information@equalityni.org
Website: www.equalityni.org

**Employers' Forum on Disability**
Telephone: 020 7403 3020
Textphone: 020 7403 0040
Email: enquiries@efd.org.uk
Website: www.efd.org.uk

**National Register of Access Consultants**
Telephone: 020 7822 8282
Email: info@nrac.org.uk
Website: www.nrac.org.uk

**Northern Ireland Executive**
Telephone: 028 9052 8400
Website: www.northernireland.gov.uk

**Royal Institute of British Architects
(RIBA)**
Email: info@riba.org
Website: www.architecture.com

**Royal National Institute of Blind People
(RNIB)**
Helpline telephone: 0303 123 9999
Email: helpline@rnib.org.uk
Website: www.rnib.org.uk

**Action on Hearing Loss (formerly Royal National Institute for Deaf People)**
Telephone: 0808 808 0123
Textphone: 0808 808 9000
Email: informationline@rnid.org.uk
Website: www.rnid.org.uk

**Scottish Government**
Telephone: 08457 741 741
Textphone: 0131 244 1829
Email: ceu@scotland.gsi.gov.uk
Website: www.scotland.gov.uk

**The Stationery Office (TSO)**
Telephone: 0870 600 5522
Textphone: 0870 240 3701
Email: customer.services@tso.co.uk
Website: www.tsoshop.co.uk

**TSO Ireland**
Telephone: 028 9023 8451
Email: enquiries@tsoireland.com

**TSO Scotland**
Telephone: 0131 659 7020
Email: enquiries@tsoscotland.com

**Welsh Government**
Telephone: 0300 060 3300
Email: wag-en@mailuk.custhelp.com
Website: www.wales.gov.uk

# Publications

### Legislation, standards and codes of practice

The Building Regulations 2000. Approved Document M: *Access to and use of buildings* 2004 Edition. Department for Communities and Local Government. The Stationery Office, 2006

The Building Regulations (Northern Ireland) 2000. Technical booklet R: *Access to and use of buildings* 2006. Department of Finance and Personnel (Northern Ireland). The Stationery Office, 2006

The Building (Scotland) Regulations 2004. 2011 Technical Handbooks: *Domestic buildings and Non-domestic buildings.* Scottish Executive. The Stationery Office, 2011

Equality Act 2010. The Stationery Office, 2010

BS EN 81-1:1998 + A3:2009 *Safety rules for the construction and installation of lifts.* Electric lifts. The British Standards Institution, 1998 (amended 2010)

BS EN 81-2:1998 + A3:2009 *Safety rules for the construction and installation of lifts.* Hydraulic lifts. The British Standards Institution, 1998 (amended 2010)

BS EN 81-28:2003 *Safety rules for the construction and installation of lifts. Remote alarm on passenger and goods passenger lifts.* The British Standards Institution, 2003

BS EN 81-41:2010 *Safety rules for the construction and installation of lifts. Special lifts for the transport of persons and goods. Vertical lifting platforms intended for use by persons with impaired mobility.* The British Standards Institution, 2011

BS EN 81-70:2003 *Safety rules for the construction and installation of lifts. Particular applications for passenger and goods passenger lifts. Accessibility to lifts for persons including persons with disability.* The British Standards Institution, 2003

BS 5655-6:2011 *Lifts and service lifts. Code of practice for the selection, installation and location of new lifts.* The British Standards Institution, 2011

BS 6440:2011 *Powered vertical lifting platforms having non-enclosed or partially enclosed liftways intended for use by persons with impaired mobility. Specification.* The British Standards Institution, 2011

BS 8300:2009 *Design of buildings and their approaches to meet the needs of disabled people – Code of practice.* The British Standards Institution, 2009

BS 9999:2008 *Code of practice for fire safety in the design, management and use of buildings.* The British Standards Institution, 2008

BS EN ISO 10535:2006 *Hoists for the transfer of disabled people. Requirements and test methods.* The British Standards Institution, 2007

*National Planning Policy Framework.* Department for Communities and Local Government 2012

*Statutory Code of Practice: Services, public functions and associations.* The Stationery Office, 2011

*Statutory Code of Practice: Employment.* The Stationery Office, 2011

*What equality law means for you as an education provider – schools.* Equality and Human Rights Commission, 2010

*What equality law means for you as an education provider – further and higher education.* Equality and Human Rights Commission, 2011

**Other publications**

*Access Audit Handbook.* CAE / RIBA Publishing, 2005. New edition due 2013

*Accessible Sports Facilities: Design guidance note.* Sport England, 2010

*Accessible Train Station Design for Disabled People: A Code of Practice.* Department for Transport and Transport Scotland, 2011

*Building Sight,* by Peter Barker, Jon Barrick, Rod Wilson. HMSO in association with the Royal National Institute of the Blind RNIB, 1995

*Changing Places: A practical guide.* MENCAP and Changing Places Consortium, 2012

*Design and access statements: How to write, read and use them.* Commission for Architecture and the Built Environment, 2006

*Easy Access to Historic Buildings.* English Heritage, 2004

*Fire safety risk assessment: Means of escape for disabled people.* Department for Communities and Local Government, 2007

*Good Loo Design Guide.* CAE / RIBA Publishing, 2004

*Guidance on the use of Tactile Paving Surfaces.* Department for Transport, 2005 (updated 2007)

*Inclusion, equality and the built environment: a glossary of terms.* The Royal Institute of Chartered Surveyors, 2012

*Home Zones: A planning and design handbook,* by Mike Biddulph. The Policy Press, 2001

*Manual for Streets.* Published for the Department for Transport by Thomas Telford Publishing, 2007

*Shared Space.* Local Transport Note 1/11. Department for Transport, 2011

*Sign Design Guide,* by Peter Parker and June Fraser. JMU Access Partnership and the Sign Design Society, 2000

*SLL Code for Lighting* (Society of Light and Lighting). Chartered Institute of Building Services Engineers, 2012

Specifiers' Handbooks for Inclusive Design:
*Architectural Ironmongery*
*Automatic Door Systems*
*Internal Floor Finishes*
*Glass in Buildings*
*Platform Lifts*
CAE / RIBA Publishing, 2005 and 2006

*Stairs, ramps and escalators: Inclusive design guidance.* CAE / RIBA Publishing, 2010

*The principles of inclusive design. (They include you.)* Commission for Architecture and the Built Environment, 2006

*Wayfinding: effective wayfinding and signing systems – guidance for healthcare facilities* The Stationery Office, 2005

**Websites**
www.homeoffice.gov.uk

The Building Regulations Part L Review
http://wales.gov.uk/consultations/planning/buildingregspartl/;jsessionid=XJ3JQyVLLsCMvH
ZNlfTzLTs4xzknlDmLHY4nY1cdLy52Pk25WZKV!-1426182689?lang=en

# Index

access audits 15
access control systems 59, 65
  car parks 22
accessible WCs 99–100
alarm buttons 87
audible announcements 115
audible signs 112
audio description services 117, 128

baby changing facilities 101, 102
BS 8300: 2009 13
building emergency alarms 99, 128, 132
Building Regulations 11–12
bus stops 34

cane detection 32
car parking 18–19
ceiling surfaces 79, 81
Changing Places (CP) toilets 102–7, 126
circulation routes 76–9
cleaning 126, 127
cross-fall gradients 28, 35
cycle parking 34, 37

design and access statements 14–15
door handles 60–1
door thresholds 50
doors
  access control systems 59
  dimensions 53–4
  entry systems 59, 66
  hold-open devices 64
  maintenance 125
  opening and closing systems 60–6
  sanitary facilities 97
  self-closing devices 62, 63
D-pull handles 60, 61
drainage, surface 28, 36
drainage channels 28, 29, 50
drop-down support rails 97–8, 105

edge protection, ramps 41

educational access 8–9
electrical power sockets 119
electronic navigation systems 112–13
employers' duties 7–8
entrances 48–9
entry systems 59, 65–6
Equality Act 2010 6–10
escape, emergency 128, 129–31
external doors 49

fire alarms 99, 128, 132
fire safety 129–30
floor surfaces 80
  circulation routes 78, 79
  entrance foyers 68
  maintenance 126
  sanitary facilities 97
fob systems 59

glare 79, 80
glazed doors 57–8, 88
glazed screens and walls 81
glazing
  circulation routes 79
grabrails 60
gradients
  pedestrian routes 27
  ramps 39
guarding
  on pedestrian routes 32, 37
  ramps and landings 41, 47

handrails 46–7
  external stairs 44
  height 47
  sanitary facilities 97, 98, 105
headroom, restricted 37
hot surfaces 98

inclined platform stairlifts 92
induction loops 72, 116
information provision

available facilities and accessibility  127–8
emergency evacuation plans  131
information signs  108, 110
internal doors  53–4
   threshholds  50
   vision panels  56

kerbs
   bus stops  34
   dropped  21, 23, 31
   lowest detectable  35
keypads
   power-operated doors  66
   telephone  114
keyways to locks  62

landings
   external stairs  44
   passenger lifts  86
   ramps  40–1
   sloping pedestrian routes  27
landmark features  108
lift landings  86
lighting  121–2
   car parks  21
   circulation routes  78, 79
   external stairs  45
   maintenance 125, 127
lobby doors  51, 52
   minimum widths  53–4
   vision panels  56
lock keyways  62
locks, sanitary facilities  97

management of building  124–8
manifestation markings  57–8, 81
manoeuvring space
   adjacent to doors  55
   in corridors  76, 77
   sanitary facilities  100, 103
matting, entrance  50, 80
means of escape  128, 129–32
multi-storey car parks  20

National Key Scheme (RADAR)  126, 128
navigation systems  112–13

noise  118
obstructions
   corridors  76
   hazard protection  30, 32, 35
   management of pedestrian routes  124
   shared spaces  35
offices  78
open-plan areas  78
outward-opening doors
   entrances  49
   grabrails  60
   on internal access routes  58
   on pedestrian routes  30

parking bays
   level of provision  18–19
   management of  124
   shared spaces  36
passageways  76–7
passing places
   corridors  76
   pedestrian routes  26, 27
   ramps  41
path dimensions  26
payphones  114–15
pedestrian routes  25–32
   hazard warning and protection  30–2
   surfaces and drainage  28–9
personal emergency evacuation plans
(PEEP)  128, 131
planting boxes  35, 38
portable ramps  42
posts and columns
   canopies  49
   entrance lobbies  51
   hazard protection  37

prayer washing facilities  101–2
projections
   entrance lobbies  51
   pedestrian routes  30, 37
protection from falling, collision and impact
12
proximity cards  59, 66
pull cords  98, 99, 107, 126
push pads  66

queuing barriers and rails  69

RADAR National Key Scheme  126, 128
radiators  98
radio systems  117
ramps
   external  39–42
   handrails  47
   temporary and portable  42
   internal  83
React system  112
'reasonable' adjustments  7, 8
reception desks  70–2
   access to  68
   queuing barriers and rails  69
reduced swing doors  51
remote infrared audible signage (RIAS)  113
revolving doors  49

safety markings  57–8
sanitary facilities  94–107
   accessible baby changing facilities  101
   alarms  99
   overall provision  94–7
seating  73–5
   entrance foyers  68
   reception desks and service counters  72
   shared spaces  36
setting-down points  24
shared spaces  33–6
   delineation  35, 36
   level surfaces (kerb-free)  35
shops  78
showers  107
signage  108–12
   braille  112
   car parks  18, 21, 22
   setting-down points  24
   tactile  111, 112
sliding doors  51, 54
sloping surfaces
   circulation routes  78
   pedestrian routes  27
soundfield systems  117–18
sports chair zones  77
stairlifts  92

steps
   external  39, 43–5
   internal  83–4
street furniture  37–8
   hazard protection  30, 35, 38
   positioning  37–8
   in shared spaces  35
strobe lighting  128, 132
surface finishes  80–2
   circulation routes  78, 79
   maintenance  126
   pedestrian routes  28
surface undulations  28
symbols  109

tactile hazard warning surfaces  30
   external stairs  45
   ramps  42
telephones  114–15
turning areas  76
turnstiles  59

vehicle setting-down points  24
vibrating pager systems  132
visibility markings  57–8
vision panels  56

waiting areas  73–5
wall surfaces  79, 81
washbasins  94, 97, 98, 106
water temperatures  98, 107
wayfinding  108–13
   electronic navigation systems  112–13
   tactile maps and models  112
widths
   corridors  76
   doors  53–4
   external stairs  44
   pedestrian routes  25–6
   ramps  40, 41
workplace access  7–8, 78